D1008579

Ordinary Women, Extraordinary Lives

How to Overcome Adversity and Achieve Positive Change in Your Life

MARCIA CHELLIS

◆ ◆ ◆

Ordinary Women, Extraordinary Lives

VIKING

VIKING
Published by the Penguin Group
Viking Penguin, a division of Penguin Books USA Inc.,
375 Hudson Street, New York, New York 10014, U.S.A.
Penguin Books Ltd, 27 Wrights Lane,
London W8 5TZ, England
Penguin Books Australia Ltd, Ringwood,
Victoria, Australia
Penguin Books Canada Ltd, 10 Alcorn Avenue, Suite 300,
Toronto, Ontario, Canada M4V 3B2
Penguin Books (N.Z.) Ltd, 182–190 Wairau Road,
Auckland 10, New Zealand

Penguin Books Ltd, Registered Offices:
Harmondsworth, Middlesex, England

First published in 1992 by Viking Penguin,
a division of Penguin Books USA Inc.

10 9 8 7 6 5 4 3 2 1

Names and other descriptive details of the individuals represented in this book have been altered in several instances.

LIBRARY OF CONGRESS CATALOGING IN PUBLICATION DATA
Chellis, Marcia, 1940–
Ordinary women, extraordinary lives / by Marcia Chellis.
p. cm.
Includes bibliographical references.
ISBN 0-670-83757-1
1. Life change events—Psychological aspects—Case studies.
2. Adjustment (Psychology)—Case Studies. 3. Courage—Case studies.
4. Women—Biography. I. Title.
BF637.L53C44 1992
158.94—dc20 91–23607

Printed in the United States of America
Set in Fournier
Designed by Joy Chu

To Bill
with thanks
for his support
and encouragement

"IT IS ONE OF THE MOST BEAUTIFUL COMPENSATIONS OF THIS LIFE THAT NO MAN CAN SERIOUSLY HELP ANOTHER WITHOUT HELPING HIMSELF."

—*Ralph Waldo Emerson*

Acknowledgments

♦ ♦ ♦

Just as making changes in one's life cannot be accomplished without the encouragement of others, this book would not have been written without the support of many people. It was a team project.

First, my gratitude and admiration go to the women whose personal stories appear in this book. They reached deep inside to bring out parts of their lives they may have preferred to keep to themselves. They willingly revealed intimate details about themselves so that others might benefit. Some wanted to use their own names. Others, for purposes of anonymity,

◆ ◆ ◆

chose different names. In those cases, I have also changed where they live and work to ensure their privacy.

I thank my agent, Jane Dystel, for her continued support. She believed in me and my commitment to this project and led me to just the right editor for this book.

It was editor Lori Lipsky's insight that readers in the nineties would need this book to show them how to process change. Endlessly enthusiastic and energetic, she guided me through the final year of writing.

Without "readers" this book would not be what it is. I'm most appreciative to my writing support group—Barbara Ackermann, Elizabeth Hunnewell, Heidi Vanderbilt, and Sally Sullivan, before she left for graduate school—whose regular meetings in Cambridge, Massachusetts, kept me on schedule. They patiently stuck with me as I struggled with the format for the book and they read every draft, sometimes more than once.

I also want to acknowledge psychologists Ivy Prescott Dwyer, Dr. Diana Kirschner, and Dr. Karen Blaker who also read pages of manuscript to comment on the psychological aspects of the women's transformations. And special thanks to Dr. Blaker and Eleanor Williams Belanger for their useful contributions to resource materials.

My appreciation also goes to Margo Baptista and Jeanne Small for carefully transcribing each interview and to Lana Lima and Melissa Perry for their secretarial assistance.

And, finally, I am grateful to my children, stepchildren, and many friends for never failing to ask how I was doing with the book.

Contents

♦ ♦ ♦

• • •

◆ ◆ ◆

A Note to the Reader

♦ ♦ ♦

Often we see public acclaim going to a celebrity—an actress, musician, athlete, or politician—who is performing once again after a severe setback or trauma such as a grave illness, a severed spinal cord, or an addiction. Rarely, however, are we given much information about what these people went through to make such remarkable comebacks. Ordinary people with similar accomplishments are sometimes more willing to reveal their vulnerabilities and the details of their struggle.

This book is a celebration of ordinary women who demonstrate unusual courage in the process of overcoming dev-

♦ ♦ ♦

astating life events. Eight women are profiled. Each chapter reads like fiction, but these stories are true. Told by ordinary women, people like us, their stories show how they turned overwhelmingly difficult circumstances into extraordinary lives.

For many who meet the challenges of the most desperate situations and rise above feelings of helplessness and hopelessness, there often comes a desire to make their triumph a gift to others. Dr. Robert Jay Lifton, author of several books on survivors from Hiroshima to the Vietnam War, referred to this concept as a "survivor mission."

To help other people avert or handle similar problems, these women *want* to share their intimate experiences and strength with others. In the final stages of their personal victories they are working in a social way to help other people overcome whatever problems they may have.

As much as we might wish it to be otherwise, we have no choice but to accept the fact that problems are a part of living. Life is actually a series of problems, which range from the seemingly inconsequential to the traumatic. No matter what our problems are—whether physical or emotional impairments, troubled relationships, uncertain careers, or the irritations of everyday life—they inevitably come tumbling over us, one after the other, in an endless flow. What the challenges are doesn't matter so much as how they are handled, which often makes the difference between a life that's miserable and one that's magnificent.

Most of us have unresolved issues and conditions that we'd like to change. Very few among us cannot gain by learning about the processes the women in this book used to succeed.

As I spent time with each one, I became increasingly aware

♦ ♦ ♦

of her "survivor mission," the hope that other women would discover something of themselves in her story and benefit from her experiences.

And that is my hope as well.

—MARCIA CHELLIS
South Dartmouth, Massachusetts

Preface

◆ ◆ ◆

While on a publicity tour for my book, *Living with the Kennedys: The Joan Kennedy Story,* I arrived late one night in Los Angeles and glanced at the itinerary for the next day. I was relieved to see a break in the routine. Instead of nonstop interviews I was scheduled to attend a Book and Author Lunch at the Ambassador Hotel at noon. Wonderful. I sent a silent thank you to the publicist for anticipating my need for this respite, a few minutes of not being "on."

The next day, after two television appearances, I arrived at

♦ ♦ ♦

the Ambassador just before noon. Walking through the lobby, I passed an easel with a poster listing events for the day and peripherally saw my picture. I stopped. Under the picture I saw the words—luncheon keynote speaker.

I was stunned. And speechless. If I had known I was going to speak, I would have gone through my usual ritual: outlines, note cards, and rehearsals. I didn't know what to do. The sponsoring group had already publicized the occasion and I just couldn't tell the chairwoman, so enthusiastically greeting guests, that her keynote speaker had no speech.

I would have to go on. I went into the ballroom and sat down at the head table. Fortunately, lunch and announcements gave me a chance to hurriedly scratch out a few notes under the tablecloth on my lap.

When I heard an introduction and my name, I walked numbly to the podium, opened my mouth, and hoped something would come out. I began with Joan's story of changing herself and her circumstances. Because of her participation in the 1980 presidential campaign, she had overturned her past image as a victim and made important changes in her life.

Following a summary of Joan's journey, I told the audience about my interest in other determined women who had changed themselves and their circumstances. I described some of the women I had interviewed who had mastered a range of situations. I said that in my next book I wanted to write about how and why they had triumphed.

The rest of what I said was a blur, but the reaction was astounding. When I finished, dozens of women from the audience spontaneously got up from their seats and came to the podium. They did not have questions about Joan; they wanted to tell me about experiences they had been through. As I

◆ ◆ ◆

listened to each one's story, I was moved by her level of sharing, her desire to reach out.

A tall, glamorous woman with long chestnut hair, wearing a scarlet red dress, stepped up in front of the group. She looked more like a Hollywood star than an author, counselor, and environmental activist. Wanting a chance to be heard, she said, "I've overcome child abuse, sexual abuse, poverty, eating disorders, divorce, and breakdown of my immune system. Now I'm helping other people get well."

I'd been impressed by all of the women, but because I was intrigued by those able to turn personal traumas into work for or service to others, I talked further with her. A few months later, I returned to Los Angeles for a series of in-depth interviews. Her story is told in Chapter 9—she's Elizabeth Rose.

But this book began long before the day I stood at that podium in Los Angeles without a speech. The seeds had started to sprout fifteen years earlier, in 1970, during the most difficult time in my life: my second child, a son, had been born seven weeks early; my husband was in the hospital on the critical list; my mother and father were both terminally ill with cancer; my marriage was floundering; and my drinking showed signs of becoming a problem. I felt helpless, overwhelmed.

For the next five years I tried to endure these trials. I nursed my son and husband to health. But, in the spring of 1971, my mother died and six months later my father died. In 1973 my first attempt to give up drinking lasted six weeks. It took two more years before I could accept—with the help of old and new friends—that I had become an alcoholic.

In 1975 I made the two hardest decisions of my life—the first was to stop drinking. Once I began to recover, everything about my life improved. I started oil painting again in my windmill studio. I played the piano. I enjoyed more time with my children. And when life's usual upsets and domestic crises occurred, I was grateful that I didn't drink, that I'd found other ways to cope.

Feeling healthy, free, and self-confident, I became strong enough to make another choice. Even though it was early in my recovery, I knew that a divorce was integral to my continued progress. But for that decision, too, I needed support. And I finally took that reluctant step.

At that point I felt I was starting my life all over again. On a very small income, I had myself to support and two children to raise and put through school. I moved to Boston to continue my career in children's television and writing. With student loans, I went to Harvard and in 1979 completed work for a master of education.

Although I felt fortunate to have made several dramatic changes, I still wasn't sure how they had happened. I thought about some of the remarkable people I knew who had disabilities but were managing their lives well. I wanted to find out what made the difference—why were some people able to handle adversity while others stayed victims? Why, for instance, out of an estimated twenty to thirty million drug dependent people, were only one to two million people recovering? What makes one person able, even eager, to triumph over obstacles while others seem more inclined to submit to defeat?

Two years earlier I had met Joan Kennedy. She was living alone and wrestling with divorce and alcoholism, the two issues I was beginning to put behind me. And just at the time my graduate work was completed, she was needed to back

◆ ◆ ◆

her husband in his bid for the Democratic presidential nomination and asked me to become her administrative assistant.

During the next three years Joan, too, began her recovery from alcoholism and ended her troubled marriage. Watching Joan's progress spurred my growing interest to understand why and how some people overcome obstacles. The revelations about change in her life and continuing curiosity about my own led me to look at other women's lives.

In 1980 I began to interview women who had shown unusual courage managing stressful circumstances. I wanted to understand this dynamic not only for myself but also for the many people who might benefit from knowing about it.

As part of my search I looked for several things: Is change possible merely by following a series of steps? Is there an event in one's life or is there something inherent in one's personality that precipitates a decision to change? What makes a person receptive to another's example or support? Do those who succeed demonstrate a common pattern? Are there skills we can learn from each other about how to change? Do those who survive or make major changes have a particular view of themselves? And, finally, if a change is made, how can it be sustained?

By 1985 I had completed dozens of long interviews with women in the Boston area—each woman the protagonist of her own incredible story. I didn't learn until later that telling their stories was actually an important part of the changing or recovering process for them.

One day I was approached by an attractive, well-dressed woman. Cindy, twenty-six, had heard about my project and began to tell me that she had been a battered wife, both verbally and physically, and had been forced to flee three times to the safety of shelters. She offered me her story and said, "It helps me to talk about it. Giving my story away makes me feel good. I can't really explain it, but it makes me feel high. I *have* to tell you what I've been through and how I survived it."

Then, while on two cross-country book tours, I met more women who wanted to be a part of the project. After a morning television talk show in Detroit I was stopped outside the studio by a woman who had just driven to the station to see me. "I woke up to your face on my television screen this morning and had to meet you." She offered to tell me her story.

In city after city I talked to audiences about women whose lives exemplified courage and a way to change. When I returned home, there were letters waiting and more arrived over the next few months.

From New York a woman wrote on yellow legal sheets: "Twenty years ago my husband abruptly left me with no money and three small sons. . . . Although I was not physically killed, I was killed in a very deep and different way. . . . I somehow survived and raised up my boys."

From Vancouver came an eight page letter on thin, blue stationery detailing a seventy-year-old woman's struggle with poverty and loneliness. She enclosed a clipping about her new job as director of a center for senior citizens and a picture of her dog. "My story shows it is possible to hit bottom and then regain usefulness and have a feeling of self-worth once again."

I answered and saved these letters. The interest of so many women encouraged me to keep going.

And I was struck by a discovery: although these women didn't know each other, they all seemed to go through the same stages on the way to recovery. It is this process that I want to share with you.

Ordinary Women, Extraordinary Lives

The Process of Self-empowerment

♦ ♦ ♦

1

To empower oneself to make successful change depends, in large part, on inviting and then responding to others' support; to sustain that change depends on giving to others a similar kind of encouragement and support. This important connection between receiving and giving support forms the basis of the **self-empowerment** process.

Receiving support can generate tremendous motivating power and even bring about a transformation in another person. But the desire to harness that power has to come first.

♦ ♦ ♦

Well-known authorities also connect an individual's capacity to resolve problems to the support they receive. Psychoanalyst Karen Horney wrote that only the individual could develop his potentialities, but favorable conditions for growth must be present. And psychologist Carl Rogers wrote that successful therapy often depends on the individual's own drive.

Therefore, I decided to call this process of recovery or change self-empowerment. Self-empowerment is about becoming powerful. It is a process to use for overcoming any barrier. It is a way to achieve personal success, a way to handle challenging circumstances, a way to make your life work. And when your life works, you have something to offer others. Once you have accomplished your objectives, you can become a role model capable of influencing and empowering someone else. When you help others to reach their goals, you become a powerful person.

Each woman in this book wants to empower others. As she moves into the final stage of self-empowerment, she finds a cause, her way of helping other people. She has a mission.

A "survivor mission" can take a variety of forms. Bernie Siegel, in *Love, Medicine, and Miracles,* wrote, "If we become survivors . . . we realize motivation becomes spiritual or selfless, not selfish. . . . We find ourselves striving for the survivor's paradoxical goal—to have things work out well for ourselves *and* others." Siegel reminds readers that out of the pain Rabbi Kushner suffered with the death of his son, he wrote *When Bad Things Happen to Good People,* helping many people through similar tragedies. In *Death in Life: Survivors of Hiroshima,* Dr. Robert Jay Lifton said that an atomic bomb survivor's efforts to contribute to "wider organic knowledge can be of help to him in mastering his own experience."

◆ ◆ ◆

By telling her story each woman in this book is gaining mastery over trauma in her past. Because she has a "survivor mission," she shares what happened to her without reservation. She wants others to identify with her—not with her particular problem but with her feelings about it and how she handled it. She wants others to learn from the process she used to change and to sense her present healthy outlook and gratitude. And she knows that by reaching out and becoming a role model, she is making a commitment to others that keeps her commitment to herself alive.

To check on the accuracy of my observations, I prepared and sent out questionnaires to several psychologists asking for their reactions and comments. I followed up the questionnaires with discussions with these and other professionals. All of them corroborated the principles of self-empowerment.

At the same time I studied material from the Harvard Medical School's Conference on Women, held in Cambridge, Massachusetts, in June of 1988, particularly with respect to lectures and papers on recovery from trauma. The papers presented emphasized that there is healing power in relationships, that connection is crucial for psychological well-being and growth, and that a receptive social network and a secure bond with another person aid in overcoming the stress of traumatic events.

Throughout this book I have cited experts in the fields of psychology and medicine. For those who would like more information in specialized areas, I have included a complete list of references at the end of the book. My sources come from books or magazines that should be readily available to you, either in libraries or bookstores.

The **self-empowerment** process has five stages: **accepting, networking, choosing, shifting,** and **mentoring.** Each stage affects individuals differently, depending upon their situation and what they want to change about themselves. A natural progression exists from the first to the last stage, although stage one and two can be worked together.

In addition to the five stages, I am also presenting four new terms: **self-value, chance to choose, positive shift,** and **empowering example**—that I will define. And to show how each stage works in people's lives I will draw examples from several additional women's stories as well as from my own experience recovering from alcoholism.

ACCEPTING

As simple as this sounds, stage one may be the most difficult—and certainly is for those with addictions. Rather than look at unsatisfactory, upsetting situations, many people prefer to use the ostrich approach: they bury the truth and hide their problems.

But recognizing weaknesses and limitations is a necessary part of living, Jean Baker Miller writes in *Toward a New Psychology of Women.* "That most valuable of human qualities—the ability to grow psychologically—is necessarily an ongoing process, involving repeated feelings of vulnerability all through life. . . . It is necessary to 'learn' in an emotional sense

♦ ♦ ♦

that these feelings are not shameful or abhorrent but ones from which the individual can move on—if the feelings are experienced for what they are. Only then can a person hope to find appropriate paths to new strengths."

Sarina, a fifty-year-old mother and former social worker, feared that her husband, a small town college professor, was molesting their adolescent daughter. Unwilling to confront him, Sarina looked the other way until her daughter broke down and confided in her—a devastating revelation. Enraged at her husband and angry at herself for not protecting her daughter, Sarina faced the problem and accepted the truth. She found help for her daughter, divorced her husband, and went back to school and to work—counseling other incest survivors and their mothers.

"Wise people learn not to dread but actually to welcome problems," M. Scott Peck wrote in *The Road Less Traveled.* "Most of us are not so wise. Fearing the pain involved, almost all of us, to a greater or lesser degree, attempt to avoid problems. We procrastinate, hoping that they will go away. . . . Problems do not go away. They must be worked through or else they remain, forever a barrier to the growth and development of the spirit."

Since problems come as part of living, why is it often so difficult to acknowledge them? Why can't people see—and say that they see—the gorilla in the living room? Why is it so hard to get past denial and face a problem head-on? Is it fear of the unknown, or is the status quo more comfortable, even if painful? Is it avoidance of the difficult process ahead, even if that could bring freedom from the current situation? Or is it uncertainty about just what the problem is?

Before I realized that my problem was alcoholism, I suffered devastating despair and remorse without knowing why. I couldn't understand what was wrong with me. Finally I made an appointment with a therapist in Boston who, after listening to me for a while, gently suggested that my problem could be alcoholism. Yes, there was alcoholism in my family, but I had hoped—and believed—that it wouldn't happen to me. And because I was a professional writer and a good mother, ran a large home, and contributed in many ways to the community, I didn't fit my own image of what an alcoholic is.

To accommodate the doctor, I decided not to drink. I reluctantly attended self-help meetings and halfheartedly listened to speakers tell what drinking had done to their lives. I heard them say how they had overcome alcoholism and relished their new way of thinking and living. Even though I couldn't relate many of their experiences to my own, I wrote down the names and telephone numbers of women who offered their help. I tucked this list under some books in the top drawer of a chest in the front hall. And for six lovely weeks I felt happy, because I wasn't drinking.

But something insidious was happening—I began to rationalize. Thirty-three was too young for a drinking problem. My friends could still drink; why couldn't I? If I didn't drink, how could I go to another wedding or dinner party? So, vowing to be careful, I returned to drinking.

Like many who resist acknowledging a situation, I must have believed that identifying and labeling the problem would make it real. I didn't learn until later that the opposite was true: acknowledging a problem, and then accepting it, marks the beginning of diminishing and resolving it.

I also learned later that denial is often the first hurdle that must be surmounted on the way to acknowledgment and ac-

♦ ♦ ♦

ceptance. If denial turns to anger over the circumstances, progress is being made. Later one sees that anger is no more than a temporary relief, and that being angry doesn't solve problems. Anger may be replaced with promises, pledges, or wishful thinking. When circumventing the issue doesn't work in those ways, the final hurdle may be depression, despair, or hopelessness.

Unfortunately there are those who have to sink to the depths and hit bottom before they are ready or able to acknowledge the seriousness of a situation or change their direction. At that point they can either face and accept the problem or live with the consequences.

To encourage acceptance of reality, Melody Beattie writes in *Codependent No More,* "Facing and coming to terms with *what is*—is a beneficial act. Acceptance brings peace. It is frequently the turning point for change."

Change becomes possible after acknowledging and then accepting the existence of a problem. There is an important distinction between acknowledgment and acceptance. Acknowledgment is admitting, being able to say that something is true. Acceptance goes much deeper. Acceptance does not mean yielding or giving up or tolerating: acceptance means receiving on an emotional level what one admits to be truth on an intellectual level.

Perhaps the best example I can give to clarify acceptance is the surrender-to-win idea that happened to me. When I was beginning to suspect a drinking problem, I could acknowledge it but not accept it. That was like throwing in the towel but still holding on to a corner. In other words, my grasp of that corner represented my reservations: it meant, to me, that maybe I didn't have a problem, maybe I could still drink like everyone else.

♦ ♦ ♦

The day I found out that I couldn't drink like everyone else was Mother's Day in 1975. It was a warm Sunday morning. My children served me breakfast in bed, then made plans for a garden picnic while my husband and I had a drink before lunch. One drink wasn't enough. I wanted another, but we were out of liquor and package stores in Massachusetts were closed on Sundays. As soon as the picnic lunch was over, I startled my husband and children by announcing that I was going to visit some friends. My real reason for going was that they always had a well-stocked bar.

As I drove down the driveway I remember looking at my hands on the wheel and thinking that they belonged to someone else. This couldn't be me—someone more interested in having a drink than staying home with her children on Mother's Day. I looked back at my children. They stood in front of the barn, trying hard to smile, waving good-bye. I didn't want to leave them, yet I was leaving. It was like watching an actress in a play. In that moment I suddenly understood what "the compulsion of the disease" meant.

Not until then, overcome by my powerlessness, could I begin accepting that I was an alcoholic. The next day I surrendered. I let go of all denial, rationalizations, false hopes, and efforts to control. Not until then, when I stopped resisting and threw in the whole fuzzy towel, was I able to begin recovery and change.

When I talked with other women in preparation for this book, I found that they too had had a moment of clarity like my driving out of the driveway, that leads to accepting a situation—exactly as it is. For some, this moment may be like looking in the mirror and seeing themselves for the first time. No longer deluding themselves by blaming someone else, "the system," or their circumstances, they usually feel relief. And hope. Hope because they know that it is up to them. No one else can take away their pain, give them happiness, or be held accountable for their successes or failures. By becoming willing to be responsible for themselves, they see that the only person who can solve their problems is the one looking back from the glass.

Accepting responsibility for one's actions doesn't mean having to solve the problem alone. Support is essential. And most people know from previous attempts that trying to make a change by oneself is difficult and often disappointing. But now they can begin to look for help from nurturing friends and begin to build a network of support.

Networking

"Get support," write Ellen Bass and Laura Davis in *The Courage to Heal.* "The environment in which you live—the people you see—affects your ability to make changes. People who are working to grow and change in their own lives will support you with encouragement and by example."

The networking stage, then, is the time to seek out appropriate assistance, to actively look for encouragement and guidance. Family members, friends, or colleagues may have suggestions. Their referrals may lead to a counselor, a clergyman, a neighbor, or someone "who has been there." Or support may come from a Twelve-Step recovery group or another self-help group, such as Recovery, Inc. One or more support people in combination with a group may work best. Once support people have been identified, they will need to know specific objectives and learn how they can help.

♦ ♦ ♦

The morning after I threw in the towel, I remembered the list of women who had offered to help me. I sat down with the list, picked up the phone, and called some of the women. I said I was ready and needed their help to stop drinking. They recalled some of their own resistance to accepting help and gently told me how their lives had been transformed by letting others support them.

During the next few months a woman named Mary insisted that I call her every morning. She asked what I was doing and what my plans were for the day. She could sense from our conversation whether or not my attitude was positive. If I needed encouragement, she gave it. Her support, especially during the first difficult days of trying not to drink, made all the difference. Turning myself over to the care and direction of someone else felt strange, but that experience eventually taught me how to direct myself.

As improbable as letting others take charge may sound at first, it is a rewarding part of the process. Other people often know better what is needed, what steps to take, and when. They can offer new input. Their caring and support often empower one to do what she or he could not do alone.

The power of support became clear for Lisa, forty-five, devastated by the death in an automobile accident of her only and cherished son. He had been a national soccer champion and an honor student. She hadn't realized how much his dreams were hers until he died. While her husband kept himself going with a demanding law practice in Atlanta, Lisa withdrew from life, put her business up for sale, and stayed in the house. Her sister Jennie, who lived in Washington, called every day, urging Lisa not to give up. Jennie also left her own four children and went to see her sister several times a month. Jennie's

♦ ♦ ♦

influence led Lisa to take down the for-sale sign, return to work as director of her business, and to start a local support group for other parents who had lost children. Even though Lisa has made great progress, the two sisters continue to talk on the phone each day.

Support elicits remarkable results not just at the beginning of self-empowerment but all along the way. Keeping in constant touch with support people is essential and makes success viable.

There has never been a time when I didn't benefit from support. Years after I'd become sober and was working with Joan Kennedy, I still needed encouragement. A friend named Sally called me several times a week. If I felt discouraged, she knew just what to say—she gave the same you-can-do-it speech more than once. She helped me to grow in sobriety, to meet the challenge of raising two children on seemingly insufficient funds, and to keep up with a demanding, nearly round-the-clock job. Sally's support, and that of other Boston women, helped me to do what I was doing.

And just recently I felt encouragement from one of the women whose story is told in this book. I was working on a final draft of the manuscript, when I received a letter from Joni. "I know you must get a little down on writing," she said, "just like I get a little down on training mega miles every day. But it is all worth it in the end. I know the book is going to be wonderful, so stay with it to the finish line."

My belief in the power of networking is corroborated by research being done at major medical centers as well as by authors writing about those who've survived trauma. At Harvard Medical School, Judith Lewis Herman, M.D. said that following an act of violence women can recover through the healing power of relationships. From Boston University's School of Medicine, Nicolina Fedele, Ph.D. and Elizabeth A. Harrington, Ph.D., who lecture on "Women in Groups: How Connections Heal," said that "relationships and connection are the vital elements of psychological growth. . . . There can be no true sense of self without the experience of healthy, healing relationships. . . ." And Dr. Bessel van der Kolk, author of two books on recovering from trauma and director of the Massachusetts Mental Health Trauma Center, said, "If victims have a receptive social support network which does not blame them for their misfortunes and can help them to mourn the loss of loved ones, or feelings of relative impotence, they are likely to recover from the trauma . . . if both internal strengths and external supports are optimally available, some sort of resolution is usually achieved. . . ."

Unfortunately, not every woman has enough internal strength to let herself respond to external support. In order for that kind of receptivity to take place, she must believe she deserves help. She needs a strong sense of self-worth.

"Self-esteem makes it possible to cope with life's disappointments and changes," Linda Sanford and Mary Ellen Donovan write in *Women and Self-Esteem.* "If a woman has an insufficient amount of self-esteem, she will not be able to act in her own best interest. And if a woman has no self-esteem at all, she will become overwhelmed, immobile and eventually will 'give up'."

Throughout this book I use the term **self-value** rather than self-esteem. To me, there is a connotation to the word self-esteem that implies too high a regard for oneself, too much self-importance. I prefer self-value because I think people do

◆ ◆ ◆

not aspire to esteem themselves as much as they simply want and need to value themselves.

For those with low self-value, there is hope. Working on improving one's self-value is possible and can be done during the networking stage. Although no one likes to admit dependence on others' admiration or approval, there is healing power in the idea that self-value is largely a reflected image. By becoming involved with others who are loving and caring, men and women can gradually come to like, and then love, themselves. Janet Woititz, author of *Adult Children of Alcoholics,* confirms in her book *Struggle for Intimacy* how important it is to be involved with people who can affirm, validate, and offer support. "A healthy relationship involves two people who give each other the right to their feelings and the sense that they are of value."

In time relationships such as this will build confidence and lead to self-approval. Healthy relationships and positive connections with other people can heal and help one to grow and change. Women in groups get in touch with their feelings and become aware of what they are avoiding and blocking out. Eventually, after sharing themselves and feeling the acceptance by others despite their faults and problems, self-acceptance grows.

Then, with an improved level of self-value, women can allow themselves to be supported in making the choices that will lead to change.

Choosing

Support people can help by pointing out that there are a number of choices for any situation, that it is not necessary

• • •

to live with compromising conditions, and that options and opportunities do exist. Being aware of the array of available choices—as well as of those people or behavior patterns that have thwarted growth—opens up the possibilities for positive change.

With the guidance of support people, chances to choose will become apparent. A chance to choose is that critical moment when a chance to make a choice or a decision appears. It is often a chance to do something beneficial. At the very least, it is a chance to do something differently. Although few act on their first chance to choose, becoming alert to these possibilities is an important part of this stage of recovery.

The idea of having choices may be new to those who are familiar with living passively, experiencing only their powerlessness. But when they learn to recognize their choices and take them, they can create their own lives.

"Once I knew that I wanted to be an artist," Judy Chicago was quoted in *Each Day a New Beginning,* "I had to make myself into one. I did not understand that wanting doesn't always lead to action. Many of the women had been raised without the sense that they could mold and shape their own lives, and so, wanting to be an artist (but without the ability to realize their wants) was, for some of them, only an idle fantasy, like wanting to go to the moon."

Women accustomed to thinking they are not capable of molding and shaping their own lives may still be clinging to a victim role, blaming others for their lot. But if they can let go of blaming others and take responsibility for their choices, they'll discover avenues not available to them when they lived as victims.

Once the idea of recognizing and making choices takes hold,

♦ ♦ ♦

there will be growth. Even euphoria. This is a time of progress. But it would be wise to prepare for setbacks, for at this time it is likely that one will make both constructive and self-destructive choices. For a while, it may even seem like two steps forward and one step backward. But setbacks and relapses are part of the process of recovering, part of the process of positive change.

Seeing a chance to choose, one might also see the risk of failure. Not only do some choices involve risk, many raise fears. There's a saying that the rewards in life are equal to or in proportion to the risks. To avoid risks and give in to fears inhibits progress. An inherent part of making choices, then, is knowing that there will not only be gains but losses, not only victory but pain.

Claire, forty-one, suffers daily with a congenital heart problem. Fending off risks and warnings about having a baby, at thirty-six she gave birth to an unusually beautiful, intelligent daughter. As much as Claire would love to have another child, she has accepted that a second pregnancy could gravely damage her health. But instead of giving up, she has been empowered by her husband's and her doctors' support. They have helped her become aware of her choices. While still considering getting pregnant, she is also looking into adoption and talking to her sister about carrying a child for her. Claire has yet to decide what she will do, but her ability to see choices gives her the power to shape her own life.

Careful, thoughtful choices define individuals, allowing them not only to reveal who they are but also to become who they can be. It's exhilarating to know this freedom—and to feel the personal power—that comes from participating in the creation, or re-creation, of one's own life.

♦ ♦ ♦

Being open to support and allowing that support to foster actions that are beneficial provides potential for this kind of self-empowerment. Making choices that contribute to one's wholeness and aliveness is energizing. Feeling good leads to other healthy choices.

Early in my recovery I had choices every day. I could use support or not. I could drink or not. These were some of my choices. I chose to accept support and not to drink. In the beginning, while trying not to drink, I wrote the days of the week across the top of a three-by-five-inch card and taped it inside a kitchen cabinet door. After each successful day, I put a check mark. One check, two checks, a week of checks.

After a month I became more sure of myself and didn't need to check off days. But I still had to be alert to my choices. Each time I went to a party I had the choice of accepting a drink or not. To prepare myself before I arrived, I practiced saying, "Club soda and a lime, please." And at home during our normal cocktail hour I had choices. I could join my husband having drinks, go for a walk, or serve dinner earlier. I tried anything to break old patterns until I finally came to a time when the battle seemed to be over.

Gradually, with every positive choice, it became easier to make another one. I began to know, almost automatically, which action to take and stopped having should-I or shouldn't-I discussions with myself. After a few months I was able to choose the best options, almost effortlessly.

SHIFTING

Then, after several months, I realized that a remarkable thing had happened: instead of trying not to drink, I no longer

♦ ♦ ♦

wanted to drink. My thinking had shifted. Relief and comfort came with shifting and my commitment to live a new way.

This part of the fourth stage I call a **positive shift.** A positive shift comes about as the result of a series of beneficial choices. The key to achieving a shift is consistency—choosing wisely time after time. After a period of making choices that build growth, confidence, and a healthy outlook, the shift takes place. It is an indication of commitment and shows up as a distinctly noticeable change in attitude and actions.

In her book *In a Different Voice: Psychological Theory and Women's Development,* Carol Gilligan uses the example of Sarah, one of the women in her abortion decision study, to illustrate the results of making a shift. In a follow-up interview Gilligan noted the change in Sarah. "I just feel strong in a way I'm not aware of having felt," Sarah said, "really in control of my life, not just sort of randomly drifting along." Gilligan augments Sarah's description of her transition, or shift. "The changes in Sarah's life and in her sense of herself are paralleled by changes in her moral judgment, which shifts from a negative to a positive mode, from 'deciding who is going to lose the least and who is going to get hurt the least' to a 'compassion' that leads to caring and respect for her own and other people's needs."

After learning to recognize and make choices, people will be closer to their goals. Their spirits lift. They may get positive feedback about their progress; they like how they feel and what is happening. The more their circumstances improve, the less they need to consider and deliberate about choice. Wanting to go forward, they will no longer vacillate and will readily make the right choices. An awareness of their unwavering commitment to results and to the change they've been working for signals that a positive shift has occurred.

From then on chances to choose will be taken with confidence. If barriers appear, they can be acknowledged, confronted, and worked around. After a shift, there are rarely setbacks and relapses, rarely a desire to return to old, less effective, ways of coping.

More than anything else, what has changed is attitude and thinking. This new way of thinking leads to new behavior. Because people who have shifted want their actions to be in harmony with their objectives, they no longer have to negotiate or reconsider each choice. They have a different point of view. They don't wonder what to do any more—they know.

As William James wrote, "The greatest discovery of my generation is that human beings, by changing the inner attitudes of their minds, can change the outer aspects of their lives."

Elsa, forty, the mother of a three-year-old girl and an editor for a West Coast publishing house, did that after she recovered from the shock of her husband's announcement that he was leaving her for another woman. Elsa held out hope for a reconciliation with help from a counselor, but her husband was not interested. He rushed through a divorce. While her thoughts wavered between revenge and frustration, she floundered. But once she accepted her unexpected role as a single working mother, she reached out to friends for support.

With friends' encouragement, she began to make choices. She read everything she could find on women in the eighties trying to juggle single parenting with careers but couldn't find enough to help her. Sometimes she felt good; other times

♦ ♦ ♦

angry. As the good times outnumbered the bad and her choices became consistently constructive, her thinking shifted.

Elsa made up her mind that she could and would handle her responsibilities. Through trial and error, she learned to balance her working life, time with her daughter, and new social activities. Following her successful change in attitude, she also shifted the emphasis on the kinds of books she edited. She actively sought out manuscripts that would help women in the nineties learn to adjust to and handle change.

As Elsa's story shows, with a positive shift there comes a new level of contentment and achievement. It is also the time for letting go of the past, for forgiving—and for knowing serenity and peace of mind.

But how does one keep these changes in place and maintain this shift?

Mentoring

The surest way to sustain a change in oneself is by helping someone else to make the changes he or she needs. Helping others is not new for women. They have been conditioned to nurture, to care, and to weave relationships.

"In general, women have been assigned to the realms of life concerned with building relationships, especially relationships that foster development," Jean Baker Miller wrote in *Toward a New Psychology of Women.* "Thus, from the study of women's lives we can begin to gain a greater understanding of growth-enhancing interactions."

How do relationships foster growth? With affirmation, one person can help another to feel self-value. Through support, one person can guide another to take positive action. By example, one person can empower another to change.

What I call an empowering example is someone whose triumph over particular circumstances is potent enough to cause a transformation in another person. Often this transformation begins when victims feel hope, perhaps for the first time, and believe that they too might change.

But why take on the responsibility of helping someone else? When an objective has been reached, why not just relax in the newness of life?

"Without constant vigilance you could resume your old ways of thinking, feeling, and relating," Robin Norwood warned in *Women Who Love Too Much.* "Working with newcomers helps to keep you in touch with . . . how very far you've come. . . . By talking about it, you give hope to others, and validity to all you went through in your struggle to recover. You gain perspective on your courage and on your life."

Thus, in the context of maintaining a positive shift, working with others is both selfless and selfish. Selfless because it comes readily to women to support and encourage another's growth. Selfish because giving away what they have received from others strengthens themselves.

When Maureen, a recovering alcoholic and a professional in the field of alcohol treatment, was particularly helpful and supportive to me, I kept thanking her for her time and ideas. "No, no," she said, "please don't thank me. You are helping me." It was a long time before I grew enough to believe she meant what she said. My stage of development reminded Maureen of where she had once been. Helping me reinforced her own growth, keeping her safely on the high plane she had reached.

♦ ♦ ♦

Later, when I was supporting other people to learn how to live without drinking, I finally understood what Maureen meant. Because I was supposed to be an example to someone else, I couldn't let down my guard; I couldn't resort to self-pity; and I couldn't ever entertain any ideas about a relapse. Because there were others who needed me to be consistent and strong, I made myself consistent and strong. Whatever help I may have been to them was returned to me—manifold.

In *Home from War* Robert Jay Lifton described a Vietnam vet who "sought to come alive via . . . a survivor mission that would enable him to cope not only with his Vietnam experience but his many levels of 'personal holocaust.'" Following a decision to become a survivor, one must "take on the 'survivor mission' of giving it form in a way that contributes to something beyond it."

In *The Broken Connection,* Dr. Lifton described Hiroshima survivors who "could reanimate their lives around peace-movement activities, which offered . . . ultimate significance within which their otherwise unassimilable experience could be understood."

Al Siebert, a psychologist and author in Portland, Oregon, who has spent more than thirty years studying the survivor personality, wrote, "People with survivor personalities are those who

—have survived a major crisis
—surmounted the crisis through personal effort
—emerged from the experience with previously unknown strengths and abilities, and
—in retrospect find value in the experience."

♦ ♦ ♦

Louise, forty-five, found value in her experience when she turned mastery over extreme physical disabilities into work for children. Bright, attractive, and with a good sense of humor, she had been born with spina bifida. When she was a child her father built motorized wagons so she could get around the neighborhood. And even though she had to heave herself forward on crutches, Louise was expected to do her share of family chores. In her early twenties, when one of her legs became infected, she had to have the leg amputated. But that didn't stop Louise. After college she became a patient advocate in a children's hospital and was elected to the National Society for Patient Representation and Consumer Affairs. Since then she has completed a graduate program to become a certified mediator and uses her skills to help children from dysfunctional families participate in decisions affecting them. She works full time, drives a car, and travels across the country to board meetings and speaking engagements. She expects no less of herself. But to those who know and see her, she is a model of courage and strength.

Like Louise, the women in this book believe that telling how they feel about their accomplishments will make a difference to those who hear them. Motivated by their individual "survivor missions," they tell us about themselves so we can apply what they've learned to our own lives.

DONNA

♦ ♦ ♦

"Why am I in this wheelchair? I don't ask anymore—I know."

2

Passengers in Donna's car sometimes ride in the backseat. I sat behind her as she drove her new gray-blue Buick toward the KVBC-TV studios in Las Vegas. Passing flashing pink flamingos and multicolored neon lights twinkling up and down both sides of Las Vegas Strip, I felt like I was in a limousine. But Donna Cline, an attractive twenty-seven-year-old blonde in a bright green silk suit, was no chauffeur. She was the anchorwoman for KVBC Weekend News and host of its weekly public affairs program, "Dimensions."

◆ ◆ ◆

When we pulled up to the curb in front of the flood-lit studio about nine-thirty that night, Donna pushed open the car door and lifted her folded wheelchair from the passenger seat. She passed it across her lap, set the wheels on the pavement by the open door, and snapped the chair open. Holding the roof of the car with one hand, she swung herself gracefully down into her wheelchair, reached for her purse, and closed the door.

I offered to push, but Donna shook her head and smiled. "I had my chair purposely designed without handles," she said, and wheeled herself across the driveway and up a ramp.

Inside the building workers nodded their hellos as she moved swiftly along the corridor to the studio being readied for her show. Glancing up at the On the Air sign to make sure it was unlit, she pushed open the studio doors and rolled in.

Lighting engineers and camera crew bustled around her set, a circular platform with a sky blue backdrop. Two workers were setting upholstered chairs next to a low round table, leaving ample room on the other side of the platform for Donna.

A bearded man in a black KVBC sweatshirt, holding a clipboard, strode toward us. Donna introduced me to her director and told him I'd be observing the show. Then she turned to him with her instructions.

"Ron, I'd like you to have one of the spots lowered. And that monitor's too close—it was distracting some of the guests last week. Are we all set with the school video? I'll introduce the guests, and then we'll cut to the clips. . . ."

As Donna finished talking two of the crew lifted her chair onto the platform. She wheeled between the two upholstered

♦ ♦ ♦

chairs as the guests took their places. She glanced quickly through the note cards on her lap, then turned and greeted her nervous guests. She leaned forward and spoke to them until they looked more at ease.

"Thirty seconds," Ron announced.

The crew maneuvered their cameras into place. From my front-row seat in the studio audience, I could see Donna and her guests on the set as well as on the monitor.

"Five seconds!" The studio fell silent.

"Good evening and welcome to 'Dimensions,' " Donna began. "Tonight our subject is learning-disabled children. My guests are . . ."

I glanced at the monitor. Many times the screen showed a full view of Donna in her wheelchair. Between segments she checked her note cards, ad-libbed with her guests and the audience. I was impressed with her warmth, her command of the subject and her rapport with the audience.

The program over, the crew lifted her off the platform. I followed at a trot as she wheeled into the newsroom and up the ramp to show me the newsdesk, where she sat to anchor the weekend news. Then she took me to the editing bay and ran tapes of her weekend news shows.

"Did you ever think you'd get this far?" I asked.

"No," she said. "For a while I wasn't even sure I'd get out of the rehab center."

The next morning, in a conference room at my hotel, we sat talking. Accustomed to asking the questions in an interview, Donna readily fell into her new role of answering them.

♦ ♦ ♦

Part of a close family, she had grown up in Indianapolis and Phoenix. Donna, two brothers, and her parents went skating, swimming, and to the beach together. "Everyone always said I looked like my mother," she recalled happily. Then her expression changed. "I wish I could have known her better."

When Donna was twelve her mother died of breast cancer. As a young girl trying to manage such an enormous loss, Donna at first refused many invitations and offers of support from friends and relatives. "I felt I could handle this on my own, and I wanted to deal with it my way. I never wanted to burden anyone with my problems."

Throughout the grief-filled year following her mother's death, Donna, her father, and two brothers stayed close and depended mainly on each other for support and strength. After a while she was able to spend time with friends and take part in the normal activities of teens.

"The next summer my friends and I went a little wild. In fact, I refused to follow my father's curfew, sneaked out of the house at night, and broke so many rules I was grounded for what seemed like most of sophomore year in high school.

"In my junior year I was upset because my father was dating. And when he remarried I got angry. I liked my stepmother, but I refused to get along with her. During my senior year we argued a lot because I didn't want anyone telling me how to run my life."

In college Donna majored in theater. She performed in school productions, found bit parts in B movies, and acted in commercials.

Back home in Phoenix and working as a waitress during Christmas break of freshman year, Donna made a new friend.

♦ ♦ ♦

Debbie lived with her mother in Nevada but was in Phoenix visiting her father. Donna and Debbie became close very quickly. "It was kind of spooky, because we were so much alike. We had so many things in common. It seemed incredible, but we even had the same birthday. I've never met anyone I hit it off with so fast."

In March Debbie decided to go back to Carson City, Nevada, to see her mother and invited Donna to drive with her. They left early one afternoon in Donna's new car for what was to have been a twelve-hour drive.

Just before midnight they were north of Las Vegas and turned into a truck stop for coffee and gas. When they pulled out Debbie was driving. Donna sat in the passenger seat and soon dozed off. But she was jolted awake by the sound of tires on gravel. She looked over and saw Debbie swing the wheel to the left, nearly hitting boulders, swerve to the right, and then lurch to the left again.

"There was like a guardian angel on the outside of the car," Donna remembered, "that told me if I wanted to live I had to get out. So I tried to open the door but, as the car started to flip over, the door closed on my left leg. I was yanking so hard trying to free my leg, I broke it. When I got the door open again I tucked myself into a ball and rolled out. I went flying across the desert in a little ball while the car turned over and over."

When she landed Donna lay on her back and heard the motor of the car still running. Her first thought was that the engine was going to blow up and she had to get over to turn it off.

"I tried to crawl, but couldn't move. I could hear Debbie

♦ ♦ ♦

on the other side of the car. She was moaning. I told her not to worry, that everything was going to be okay, that somebody would come for us."

The night was clear and cool. Now and then Donna would hear Debbie's moans. She tried to reassure her friend, but she was drifting in and out of consciousness. They had been listening to a tape of The Alan Parsons Project and it kept playing. Whenever Donna regained consciousness she heard the same songs over and over.

"The next thing I knew a truck driver was leaning over me. He took blankets out of my car and covered me. Then I saw flashing red lights and another man standing over me."

Donna was lifted onto a stretcher and carried to the ambulance. After a while they brought in Debbie, her cut and swollen face almost unrecognizable under the glaring white light inside the ambulance.

During the hour ride Donna kept talking to her friend. "It's going to be okay. We'll be fine." Debbie could only make sounds.

At the hospital X rays revealed that Donna had a broken back. Debbie's injuries were thought to be less critical because the attending physician didn't realize she had a punctured lung. The doctors didn't expect Donna to live and operated on her right away.

The next day, when she opened her eyes, Donna was lying in intensive care. Her bed was a machine that rotated from side to side to improve her circulation. She couldn't move.

Her father was standing over her, holding her hand, and smiling. "How am I? Donna asked him. "What's going to happen?" Her father repeated what the doctor had told him —she was lucky to be alive, but her back was broken. She

♦ ♦ ♦

tried to move her legs. When she couldn't Donna told herself that as soon as they took her out of the machine she'd be fine.

Later Debbie's mother came in the room and hugged her. Eagerly, Donna asked how Debbie was. Debbie's mother told her that during the night her daughter had died. Donna began to cry.

"Suddenly it didn't matter anymore that I couldn't move my legs. The only thing I cared about was losing my close friend."

Donna was taken to a medical center in Reno and for the next four weeks she lay flat on her back, medicated with pain killers. When doctors thought she was ready they let her go by air ambulance to a rehabilitation center in Phoenix.

The next day Donna was put into a wheelchair and pushed out to the patio to meet the other teenagers who lived at the center. "They were all permanently paralyzed. And they were talking about what had happened to them—a car accident, a diving accident, surfing. I never identified myself with them. I thought I'd be okay. I'd been told countless stories of people with broken backs who were fine and walking again. I fully expected that it was only a matter of time before I would walk, too.

"After I'd been at the center awhile and spent a lot of time with the other kids, all of them in wheelchairs, one day the truth finally dawned on me—I was just like them, I was always going to be in a wheelchair. I suddenly understood—this was going to be my life.

"When I finally accepted that I'd never walk again, I didn't

◆ ◆ ◆

consider giving up or think of suicide. But I wasn't sure what I could or would do. Who would be my friends? What would people think of me? Would my boyfriend Roger still like me? Could I have sex? Would I ever dance, or play sports, or act again? Where would I live? How could I manage the rest of my life in a wheelchair?"

Struck abruptly by tragedy, it was natural for Donna to wonder whether life was fair and ask herself, why me? As many of us do at some point in our lives, she eventually discovered that the answer to why me is, why not me?

She began her recovery with the first stage of self-empowerment by accepting the seriousness of her condition. Her life would never be the same. She had a handicap she would have to deal with. Usually optimistic, Donna had been reluctant at first to make such statements, to her they seemed like giving up. Although she could see for herself that she couldn't walk and she'd heard her doctors' pessimistic prognoses, she hadn't been ready to hear or to bear the truth.

People cannot reach a deep level of acceptance until they are ready. Some have to "hit bottom" before they can face the inevitable. When Donna became strong enough physically and psychologically, she was able to accept that her paralysis was permanent.

Although the manner of accepting loss may vary for each of us, we can learn from what Donna did. To get to acceptance, she had to go through a difficult and painful process of grieving her loss. For the first few months she sustained herself on denial. She refused to believe she'd have to spend her life in a wheelchair. When that prospect appeared to be her destiny,

◆ ◆ ◆

her denial turned to anger. Frustrated and upset, she asked herself again and again, "Why me? Why did this have to happen to me?" Her anger reemerged as fear—fear that she could no longer do things for herself or by herself. Then, as sometimes happens in the grieving process, her fears gave way to hope once again. She made promises to herself: "If I do everything they tell me in physical therapy, I'll be able to walk again." Yet no matter what promises she made to herself or her therapist, or how hard she tried, she remained paralyzed.

In the face of what she considered to be an unbearable situation, Donna slipped into depression. She felt helpless and hopeless. In despair and believing she had lost her life as she knew it, she withdrew from the others at the rehabilitation center and refused to socialize or participate in activities.

It might have helped her to know why this kind of depression occurs. "Feeling that present conditions and future possibilities are intolerable," Bernie Siegel wrote in *Love, Medicine and Miracles,* "the depressed person 'goes on strike' from life, doing less and less, and losing interest in people, work, hobbies, and so on." Siegel observed depression in people who had experienced a sudden or drastic change or loss that leaves them feeling powerless.

Paradoxically, it was that feeling of powerlessness that eventually led Donna to accept her present situation and cope with the uncertainty of her future. She stopped fighting her reality. She completed the pain of grieving her losses—independence, a carefree life-style, the use of her legs. At that point, she came to acceptance and was able to say, "This is it."

Ironically, by letting go of denial and control, acceptance propels us forward. Donna was only twenty, but she was ready. She felt lucky that she had already achieved a degree of independence, that she had become accustomed to making decisions and to running her own life. Now that energy would have to go into taking responsibility for herself in a different way, for managing her life with limitations. She knew no one could do it for her; the onus of making progress would be hers. She became willing to do whatever was necessary to have her life work.

And one of the first things she had to do was accept the necessity of being dependent on others, for a while at least. Donna began to look for people to help her—to give her encouragement and support, to show her new ways to do things, and to be role models for her. This initial dependence would move her toward becoming independent, once again.

Each day Donna worked with Brad, a medical student who was doing part of his training in physical therapy at the center. He taught her how to get from the floor into her chair by herself. He showed her how to build strength in her upper body and how to do everyday things in a different way. Later, when Donna was able to get around with braces, she and Brad went for walks and out to lunch together.

Roger, the young man Donna had been dating, often drove to the center to visit her. He took her out on weekend passes, praised her rapid progress, and became even more caring than he had been before the accident.

"Roger was being real sweet, but he was seeing me as the person I was before the accident. I didn't want to hurt him, but I felt that Brad accepted me as I was and that he would encourage me to do more. I thought Roger would be solicitous and, if I went with him, I might stay dependent. It was very difficult and sad, but I finally decided to tell Roger that I was going to go out with Brad.

"Brad was three years older than I was and very handsome. In fact, some of the nurses seemed jealous when I started seeing him."

When Donna was ready to leave the center, her father told her he didn't think she should live at home. He felt that Donna would be dependent on him and her stepmother and that it would be to her benefit to live on her own. At first she felt stunned and hurt. But as she thought more about their decision, she was able to agree. If she were at home, she could count on them and might never learn to take care of herself. But the idea of finding a place to live by herself was terrifying.

The nurses knew she needed an apartment and one of them invited Donna to move in with her. Her house was one-story, with a patio and pool, surrounded by hibiscus bushes and grapefruit trees. There was a small apartment attached to the house, and she offered it to Donna. Donna's Social Security insurance checks were sufficient to pay the rent and she gratefully accepted the offer. Brad helped her move in and then, a few weeks later, he moved in too.

As pleasant as her new surroundings were, Donna found it hard to be away from the ramps, wide hallways, and smooth surfaces at the center. She abruptly became aware of all the places she couldn't go and all the things she couldn't do.

"I had to keep trying and to learn new ways of doing things. Brad taught me a lot, but the most important thing he taught me was that I could do almost all the things I had before—I just had to do them differently."

◆ ◆ ◆

With insurance money she had been awarded after the accident, Donna bought a van. Brad lifted her into the passenger seat or picked up the wheelchair and rolled her into the back of the van.

When she was with Brad nothing seemed impossible. She didn't have to decide whether or not to try things—he announced where they were going and Donna went. They drove up to the mountains and stayed in a cabin. They drove to Colorado and visited Brad's relatives. In a small alpine ski town they sledded down the mountain. His optimism and energy kept Donna going.

Eventually the subject of marriage came up. The weekend Brad's sister got married, they went to Palm Springs and stayed with his parents. "That's when we really started to talk about getting married," Donna recalled.

In the second stage of self-empowerment Donna was networking to find the support and help she needed. By entrusting herself to others she was helping herself to grow and heal.

Not everyone can turn herself over to the care of others for guidance and direction in this healthy way. There may be some people who allow themselves to become dependent but then don't grow beyond that stage. But Donna had the capacity to respond to people who offered their help and to benefit from the experience of being supported. She was so enthusiastic that she gained incentive, confidence, or skills from nearly every person whose life touched hers.

Donna readily made use of others' support because of one

essential factor—she had a strong sense of herself. Having a positive self-value to start with made her recovery easier.

Many of the ideas we have about ourselves in adulthood come from how we were treated and what others told us about ourselves when we were young. Over time we internalize this information and come to view ourselves the way others see us. The love and validation Donna had received from her family growing up helped her to believe in herself, enabled her to love and feel confidence in herself, and resulted in high self-value. Because she considered herself worthy and valuable, she was able to take care of herself in important ways. At that time one of those ways was to be supported by others.

Loving relationships can bring about miracles. By sharing with and caring about someone else, one person can motivate another far beyond expectations. This is true not only for building another's self-value, which I will talk about in the next chapter, but also for bringing about achievements.

Many benefits result from involving other people while we try to change our circumstances or ourselves. At these times we often do not know what is best for us. There may be possibilities and ideas that we do not think of. Another person might urge us to try the things we've avoided and dreaded, perhaps the very things we need to make progress. Hence, a healthy dependence can lead us to independence, as it did for Donna.

Donna's high self-value enabled her to welcome help from Brad, Roger, and the nurses. Brad, more than anyone, empowered Donna. When he showed her a new skill or suggested she attempt something difficult, Donna was motivated to try.

The more receptive she was to the support of others, the

stronger she grew. The more willing she was to take their suggestions, the faster she progressed. And the more responsive she was to others' examples, the more independent she became.

As a result of networking, she moved into the next stage, choosing. Each day there were choices to make, and Donna became aware of and alert to hers.

While Brad was at work Donna took care of household chores. She cooked by putting the cutting board or bowls on her lap. Wheeling herself from one side of the bed to the other to tuck in sheets and blankets, she made the bed. Vacuuming was a challenge because she had to move herself and the vacuum cleaner at the same time. But when the house was clean, she rewarded herself with a swim in the pool.

One day Brad arrived home for dinner but announced that he was going right out again to play racketball. Donna was upset. "I wish *I* could play racketball," she said. She had loved the game. She felt so frustrated she wanted to rip the arm off her chair and throw it across the room. "Are you just going to leave me here?" she shouted.

"If you want to play, come and play," Brad said.

That day she watched. The next time she rolled out onto the court. With one hand on the wheel and the other holding the racket, she was hitting some shots within minutes, spinning the chair and swinging hard at the low-flying ball.

After that she played racketball regularly. She took up tennis. And because Brad worked out with weights, Donna started lifting, too.

♦ ♦ ♦

One night after dinner, as they sat on the bed talking, Brad asked, "Do you want to do this all your life? Don't you want to go back to school? Don't you want to *do* something?"

At first Donna worried that she was becoming a burden to Brad. But she realized he was right—she did want to do more with her life. She considered whether she should go to school or get a job. Either way, she would have to learn to manage the van by herself. Although her van had been equipped with hand controls, she had driven only when Brad was with her.

Donna remembered the day, a few weeks earlier, when a friend from the center had come to the house to visit. "I watched her get out of her wheelchair and climb up into my van. It was an incredibly high transfer, and I was afraid she was going to fall. I started to feel guilty about Brad just sweeping me up and placing me in the seat."

So while Brad was at work one hot summer day—the temperature had soared to 110 degrees—Donna went out to the van alone and slid open the door. She maneuvered herself from the chair onto the floor in back. Dripping with sweat, she reached out for the wheelchair but then quickly pulled back her hand. The metal frame of the van was scorching hot. She found a piece of towel and covered the metal so that she wouldn't burn herself. She tugged and tugged until she had hauled the heavy chair inside. She scooted around, positioned the chair so it wouldn't roll over on her, and raised herself off the floor into the driver's seat.

Exhausted, Donna sat shaking for a few minutes. Then she drove to the nearest shopping mall, parked, and practiced

♦ ♦ ♦

getting herself and the chair in and out of the van. By the time she returned home, she thought she felt as tired as someone who had run the Boston Marathon.

With this accomplishment Donna felt confident enough to call the agent who had gotten her acting parts in college. He promised to look around and call her back.

In the presence of overwhelming circumstances people often cannot see their way out. They may be blind to the fact that in every situation they have choices. Yet in some instances, options may not be apparent or the role of victim may be a familiar one. For some, being a victim not only feels comfortable, the role also yields such payoffs as attention, sympathy, and self-pity. But not for Donna. She was well on her way to recognizing the choices she had and to making beneficial ones.

Now at the third stage, she was choosing to make good use of her opportunities whenever they appeared. For example, when Brad left her to play racketball she had choices: she could stay home and sulk; she could get angry at Brad when he returned; she could try the game herself. Her choice was to seize the moment and learn to play racketball in her chair. And again when she considered that she couldn't go anywhere in the van without Brad, she had several choices: she could use fear as an excuse to do nothing; she could expect Brad to dote on her; she could learn to drive the van by herself. Donna chose to go out and teach herself how to manage the van alone.

Thus, even when it doesn't seem like it, choices are always

♦ ♦ ♦

available. In any given moment, we have chances to choose. But it's up to us to decide which choices are in our best interests.

As Donna continued recognizing her options and choosing positive actions, she grew closer to the fourth stage, shifting.

Donna's agent did extensive searching before he called her back. His report was definite. "There are no parts," he said, "for people in wheelchairs."

Donna was discouraged and didn't know what to try next. Then, several weeks later, it occurred to her—radio. Why not? No one could see her; she'd be judged on her voice alone. She enrolled in broadcasting school.

"I was the only girl in the school," Donna recalled. "We had a lot of taping to do and I was constantly getting calls from the guys to plan our projects.

"The calls put a lot of strain on my relationship with Brad. He was extremely jealous of the calls and we hardly saw each other anymore. He had finished med school and was working as an intern. When we had a party at our house and all the pretty nurses he was working with came, then it was my turn to be jealous."

Donna and Brad talked about their changing relationship. As Donna became more independent and self-reliant she was less dependent on him. It was a difficult time of adjustment for both of them. Even though it appeared that their relationship had changed too much to recover, the thought of giving up Brad was too painful for Donna to accept easily.

Brad had made her feel attractive. He had restored her confidence. He had been the catalyst for her learning physical skills, stabilizing her emotionally, and motivating her professional ambition.

Finally, after many conversations and making the decision to go separate ways, Brad moved out and Donna stayed in the apartment. For weeks after Brad left, Donna suffered the enormous pain of losing someone she had loved deeply. She felt alone, afraid, and unsure of herself. She doubted that anyone else would find her attractive or that she would ever have another romantic relationship. She wondered how she would manage without him. But she would always credit Brad for the remarkable progress she had made.

Debbie's mother, who had kept in touch with Donna, reassured and comforted Donna through this loss. Then, when she thought Donna was ready, Debbie's mother urged Donna to consider television.

Donna experimented with a brief pilot segment on closed-circuit television at broadcasting school. Instructors and fellow students told her that she was "a natural." "And I made up my mind that that's what I wanted to do."

She cut a demo tape and sent it to a number of television stations along with job applications. Over the next few weeks, however, all her applications were rejected.

Discouraged, Donna drove to Mesa, Arizona, moved in with a friend, and found a job selling advertising space for a newspaper.

One day, while flipping through a *Ms.* magazine at the grocery store, she read a story about Susan Auday Fisher, a

♦ ♦ ♦

reporter at an NBC station in South Carolina. Ms. Fisher had become the country's first woman TV anchor in a wheelchair. Donna rushed to a phone and called South Carolina. She told Ms. Fisher that she was a role model for her and how much it had helped to read her story. By the end of the conversation, both women were crying. Donna was excited. She felt hope and new possibilities for herself.

"Now I know," she thought after the call. "I know I can do it."

By shifting to a level of commitment and belief in herself, Donna had come to the fourth stage of self-empowerment. She had been helped by an empowering example, someone who had "been there" and was capable of motivating Donna to go on.

Now no longer questioning whether she'd make it in television, Donna was sure that she could and that she would. She had no doubt about her intentions; she had no need to wonder whether or not to take a chance to choose. If an option would move her closer to her goal, she took it. After making a series of productive choices, she made a positive shift that was reflected in her attitude, direction, and actions.

How did Donna know she'd made a shift? How could she tell?

After a time of making beneficial choices, something happens, something in us changes. We can feel it as an inner peace. We can sense it as sureness, clarity, certainty. Our direction has become clear to us. We are focused. We know where we are going. We know what we want to achieve. Our choices take us in the direction we want to go; our actions are consistent; our vision is within reach. Above all, we have a firm commitment to that vision.

To get a sense of what making this kind of commitment does to our progress, let's look at some possible projects, objectives you might be considering for yourself or are already working on, to see what happens after a positive shift is made. For example, if your goal is to lose weight, you will be able to refuse dessert and not bring home a pound of fudge. If you have a commitment to get physically fit, you may argue with yourself about whether or not you feel like working out, but you'll get dressed and go. If your intention is to live without drugs, you'll know how to handle a situation where they are available.

How do these actions differ from choosing? During the third stage you make some good choices and some bad. From time to time you may have a setback. You buy the fudge, sleep through a few morning runs, and try drugs again. Then, as soon as you can, you'll make the choices that put yourself back on track again.

When you get to stage four, shifting, you'll have gone past the time when having setbacks is a normal part of the process. Although your thinking may waver occasionally and you may even entertain a return to previous self-destructive ways, after making a positive shift you won't give in. You'll be strong. Your mind is made up and that solid commitment will get you through those ever-present temptations to regress. You'll like doing what's best for you and feel good about it.

Donna, too, liked having a commitment to a goal. She knew a career in television wouldn't be easy, but she was on her

• • •

way. And when she achieved her objective, she would discover, quite unexpectedly, another purpose for her life.

When Donna had sent out her first round of applications for a job in television, one rejection letter had come from the news director in Flagstaff, Arizona, who had suggested that if Donna were ever in the area she should stop by. This was enough of an invitation for Donna, who drove her van to Flagstaff.

At the station she introduced herself to the news director. He showed her around, and when they got to the newsroom, she volunteered to write some wire stories for the evening broadcast.

Within a week, she was offered a job—anchor for the weekend news! She started a few weeks later.

"They didn't have a ramp to the set," Donna recalled. "Until one was built the sportscaster carried me up the steps and I sat in a normal chair.

"The news director worked with me the first weekend, showing me how to produce the show. The next weekend he turned me loose. I'd never done it before, but I wrote the script, pulled the video, and made a lot of decisions. It was great."

Donna applied to Northern Arizona University in Flagstaff to study for a bachelor of science in telecommunications. With help from her friends, she moved into a college dorm. And within a few weeks she was going to classes, anchoring the college's weekly cable show, and anchoring the weekend news for the station in Flagstaff.

During her second year at the Flagstaff station, she was

♦ ♦ ♦

promoted to weekday anchor. Her work made her more visible and, at first, she felt uncomfortable being recognized in public places. Gradually she became accustomed to her role as a public figure and was flattered when Mary Jo West, a popular news anchor from the CBS affiliate in Phoenix, asked to do a story on her.

"Mary Jo's story ran on 'CBS Nightwatch.' After that, we became really good friends. She, too, was a role model for me. I needed a lot of professional guidance and she advised me. She told me to write my scripts to fit the video, to make my words describe the pictures. She told me to lose weight, that looks were important. And she said to get into a bigger market soon."

After two years as the weekday anchor in Flagstaff, Donna thought she was ready for a move to a larger city. She hired an agent who sent tapes of her broadcasts to stations in the south and southwest. Then, for the next two months, she made follow-up calls while she waited anxiously and hoped for a positive reply from one of them.

Three months later one news director called. He was from a station in Las Vegas.

"How would you like to be a reporter and begin as back-up anchor for the weekend news at KVBC-TV in Las Vegas?" he asked.

"I'd love it!" Donna said instantly.

As she accepted his offer she thought, "Las Vegas! Wow! I can't believe it. I've made it to the big time."

♦ ♦ ♦

After seeing Donna on the air for several months the Governor's Committee invited her to enter the Ms. Wheelchair Nevada Pageant. She agreed only after she'd been convinced that it was not a beauty contest and that her participation could benefit others with disabilities.

At the pageant Donna was asked questions publicly and then interviewed privately by a panel of judges to determine what she knew about issues related to the disabled. A team from her station was there to support her and to cover the event. She had thought so little about the competitive aspects of the event that she was caught off guard by the results. She won and became Ms. Wheelchair Nevada.

From there she went on to the national contest for Miss Wheelchair America held at the Roosevelt Institute for Rehabilitation in Warm Springs, Georgia. The night of the Governor's Ball, Donna wheeled herself with her military escort, her father, and her stepmother under willow trees lining the formal garden paths into the southern plantation.

While the band played and soft light from crystal and silver chandeliers lit the ballroom, Donna danced in her chair while her escort, Bob, danced in front of her. For slow dances she used a larger chair with enough room for Bob to sit on the edge of the chair. And, for the first time in her life, she danced with her father.

Donna did well enough in each segment of the competition to become a finalist. On the last night, in a dark blue evening gown, she sat on stage with four other women in wheelchairs waiting to hear who had won. The fourth, third, second, and

♦ ♦ ♦

first runners-up were announced. Then she heard, "Our new Miss Wheelchair America is Donna Cline!"

"I screamed. Everybody screamed. Last year's winner and the director put a sash on me and balloons cascaded from the ceiling. It was the most exciting night of my life."

And it may also have been the most important. Up to that point Donna's personal and professional accomplishments had been outstanding. But with this new responsibility her life took on another, far more meaningful dimension.

Donna began to act as a spokesperson for those with handicaps. She traveled by herself across the country making appearances: "Sally Jessy Raphael" in St. Louis, "Today" in New York, "People Are Talking" in San Francisco.

"When they asked what I considered were the biggest barriers, I told them attitudinal barriers, because physical barriers can be overcome with just a little manpower.

"I told them that people with disabilities don't all live at home. They don't all need help to do everything. We are normal people. We can achieve or we can do nothing. We can get married and have kids. We are just normal people and want to be accepted that way."

Some of the audiences Donna spoke to were people with handicaps. To them she said, "I know you look out and say 'ugh,' because society is so against you. You don't know how to tackle it and you don't want to. But you have to, if you want to live normal lives."

She told them she knew what it was like because for a while

she had stayed home and received government checks. "Don't be afraid to take chances," she told them, "or to risk having doors slammed in your faces. I want you to go out there and make possible employers feel comfortable with you."

She wanted to go to Washington to discuss the needs of the handicapped with President Ronald Reagan. With help from local officials, she was able to set up a meeting.

At the White House, Donna told the president how important she thought it was to get disabled Americans back to work, to give them training so they could become contributing members of society, and how new programs and attitudes could stop the drain on our Social Security system.

She talked about her dream for a barrier-free society. "There is nothing worse," she told the president, "than someone who wants to go back to work and who has the qualifications but can't get up the steps."

A few months later Donna received a telegram from President Reagan, inviting her to return to Washington. At a press conference that included issues of interest to the disabled, Donna positioned herself in the front row. She wanted to be seen and to ask questions. At the end of the press conference, presidential aides invited her to the lunch in the state dining room and seated her next to the president.

From that time on Donna worked on rights for the disabled. She produced public service announcements on handicapped parking. She helped to push through a bill for having a National Barrier Awareness Day and she assisted in forming the National Barrier Foundation. She became part of an effort to get the Americans With Disabilities Act in motion, a bill that would protect the nation's forty-three million deaf, blind, lame, and variously impaired people against job discrimination and provide them with access to transportation, shopping malls, office buildings, and other public places.

Capable of motivating and influencing other people, Donna had emerged as a role model. "Traumatized persons need to abandon their identity of being a victim," Bessel van der Kolk wrote in *Psychological Trauma.* "This requires active reexposure and attention to other people's lives, interests, and difficulties."

As Donna helped others in the fifth and final stage, mentoring, she also strengthened herself. Knowing that other people looked up to her reinforced her commitment to herself to keep on keeping on. She became able to do for other people what Brad and Susan Auday Fisher had done for her. Donna's visibility makes it possible for her to work with and for many people at once. Her goal is not only to change public attitudes toward those with handicaps, but also to urge those with handicaps to become responsible for themselves and to do as much with their lives as they wish. The disabled identify with her struggle and know that she understands their problems. Listening to Donna, they feel hope and, watching her, they imagine themselves achieving more.

Being a role model gives Donna purpose. This role benefits her as much as it does others. She has to maintain a positive outlook, cannot let herself slip into self-pity, and cannot give up in any way without letting down all those who look to her as their model or empowering example. Because she believes her example can make a difference to someone else, she wants to help as many people as she can.

♦ ♦ ♦

Those who overcome a misfortune often find their continuing success depends on turning it into a benefit for others. This gift is part of the survivor's mission. As Nietzsche wrote, "He who has a 'why' to live can bear almost any 'how.' "

Since we met, Donna has moved to a larger city in the Midwest and been promoted to weekday anchor. She continues to excel professionally and to work for the disabled.

At the end of our last session together she said, "If it hadn't been for the accident I wouldn't be doing the work I'm doing or be the person I am today. I feel chosen and lucky to know why I'm here. Why am I in this wheelchair? I don't ask anymore—I know.

"And giving me the ability to walk isn't going to change much—except that it might improve my tennis game a bit."

L A U R E N

♦ ♦ ♦

"I have so much to lose now if I go back to heroin and hooking."

3 "On the streets of Tampa I charged fifty dollars for intercourse and twenty-five for oral," Lauren said. "Sometimes I dressed up and went to bars at the airport so I could charge more."

Lauren's words belied her appearance. In her early thirties, she wore a tailored navy suit and carried a briefcase. She was interested in becoming part of my project and began to tell me about herself as we walked near the State House in Boston. I glanced at her shiny dark hair, clear brown eyes, and healthy

◆ ◆ ◆

complexion. It was hard to believe she was talking about herself.

For a moment the sound of her words seemed to make her retreat. She may have been reminded of growing up in a large Victorian house south of Chicago, the pampered, only child of adoptive parents. "I did it only when I had to," she said softly. "I wasn't doing it steady.

"But I'd become a heroin addict and needed the money. Sometimes I'd go up to New York to sell drugs, and then I wouldn't have to hook for a while." Prostitution had led to her arrest and several months in a Florida jail. After her release she ended up in a shelter for street people.

Once again her voice grew strong. She stood a little taller and looked self-assured when she talked about her present life.

"Today I'm an advocate for women. I'm going to law school so I can be more effective with my advocacy work. And I'm very happily married."

Why had this young woman slid to such depths, I wondered, but knew I would have to wait until I'd heard the whole story for the answers. Even more, I wanted to know what she had done to save herself, how she had managed to reverse the spiral.

During that first meeting she told me only the main points of her experience. Many days later, when she finished telling her story, I had a chance to think about it. There were several times when she might have started the self-empowerment process, but she couldn't. Later I came to understand why. And when I did, I realized that Lauren's delays and missteps would make her story that much more valuable to others.

Throughout her story there are ample chances to see the

consequences of denial and of spurning support. And when she misses cues to change, she adds what seems like scene after senseless scene to her saga. But by following her long, agonizing descent, we can learn as much from Lauren as we do from Donna. Donna's story shows how high self-value can produce a smooth, dramatic denouement, while Lauren's story illustrates how low self-value can thwart recovery and change. Perhaps the greatest value in Lauren's story is the opportunity she gives us to witness and identify with procrastination, undoubtedly a common phenomenon.

From the time she was two, Lauren worried that her adoptive parents wouldn't keep her. They'd adopted a second daughter with several physical defects and returned the infant to the adoption agency.

"From then on, no matter how much they said they wanted me, I never believed them. I was sure they'd take me back, too."

Lauren's parents tried to reassure her. Her mother dressed her in ruffled dresses and called Lauren her "Little Doll." Overweight and wearing glasses, she didn't feel like a "Little Doll." Her father was busy with his business and paid little attention to her.

Lauren wanted to play with neighborhood children, but her parents thought other children would be negative influences and kept her in the house. With a book and a plate of cookies, she sat day after day in a window seat reading. She was allowed out only to go to museums or to the library.

"The best part of the day was my grandmother's visit. She helped me do homework, paid for ballet lessons, and bought

◆ ◆ ◆

me a violin. In her eyes I never did anything wrong. And when she died my whole world collapsed. I felt abandoned."

Growing up, Lauren longed for friends. She wanted to be like the other girls in the neighborhood who wore sheaths, danced the twist, and listened to the Beatles. But she could only listen to classical music. While other teens had boyfriends, Lauren never had a date in high school.

"I wanted desperately to be a hippie, but I was too timid." Her rebelliousness showed at first in small, symbolic gestures—an Indian shirt, her hair ironed straight, long dangling earrings. Later she fought openly with her father, a man who seemed to her to be uncaring and indifferent and came out from behind his newspaper only to reprimand her for her opinions. After a fight with him she would stomp off to her room and defiantly listen to Janis Joplin or the Doors.

Lauren was sent to small private schools where her advanced reading skills put her ahead of classmates. Bored by class level assignments, she neglected them and was incorrectly labeled a slow learner. When she told the school guidance counselor that she wanted to be a lawyer, he said, "You don't have the brains." Lauren believed him.

After graduation from high school she enrolled in a college program to become a physical therapist, as her grandmother had been. But she was terrified by the university setting. In her freshmen year she gravitated toward the first group of students who acted friendly. They offered to teach her how to smoke pot. She was afraid her parents would find out, but she wanted friends so badly she learned.

One day, in the cafeteria before physics class, a new girlfriend handed her a cup of coffee. Touched by the friendly gesture, Lauren took the cup. An hour later in class the room

♦ ♦ ♦

swayed and the letters on the blackboard waved in and out. Lauren didn't know that her friends had put mescaline in her coffee. When she found out, they said they were just helping because she'd never try it on her own.

After a while she began to like drugs. She thought they gave her confidence and made it easier for her to be with other students.

Aware of Lauren's eagerness to have friends, a young man from her math class invited her to his apartment one afternoon. He introduced her to gin and to sex. She liked alcohol but hated sex and wondered what the other girls were raving about.

At a Christmas party that first year Lauren's efforts to look like one of the group failed. She stood at the bar and drank so many manhattans she threw up. Another student drove her home. That night she sat in the living room with her parents, trying not to get sick again, and listened to them. "You were raised better than this!" her father said, and pounded his fist on his knee. "How could you do this to us?" Lauren held her throbbing head between her hands. "Please don't drink anymore," her mother pleaded.

But the next year, while training in a hospital physical therapy program, she continued to drink and use drugs. She noticed that her personality was changing. She wasn't timid anymore. She began using four-letter words. She became hostile when expressing her political views. She was so disagreeable that her supervisors requested several times that she get control of herself.

Finally Lauren was dropped from that hospital's training program. She ignored the implications of her dismissal and what drugs were doing to her. Instead she rationalized about the new program she'd found.

♦ ♦ ♦

"The new hospital was terrific. There were twenty-five men and only one other woman, Jodie. Jodie and I wore white miniskirts in the lab and she told me who was good in bed, who smoked, who drank, and who did drugs."

Jodie invited Lauren to live in the Lake Shore Drive apartment her parents were paying for, to use her Cougar convertible and charge cards. Every night on their way home from the hospital the girls stopped at bars on Rush Street and invited men home with them.

"It became musical beds. Sex was better than I'd thought. We dated married doctors who put us on the pill. I weighed 120 pounds, and the pill gave me boobs. And, with contact lenses, I finally felt pretty.

"Jodie and I grew pot on the balcony in plastic tubs. We took uppers to stay awake, downers to get to sleep, and speed for our weight. We did hash and cocaine. At the time, we thought it was great."

After graduation her parents urged her to move back home. But Lauren couldn't give up the city's razzle-dazzle until she had a crisis. She and Jodie were dating football players from the Chicago Bears. But Lauren was so unsure of herself with this crowd she thought she needed even more drinks and drugs to keep up.

Not only Lauren's parents, but Jodie, too, grew concerned. She urged Lauren not to drink so much.

"Why not?" Lauren asked.

"Because you get into arguments. Because you don't know when to drop a subject, especially politics. And because you're spoiling the good times. Mellow out."

Lauren nodded and lit a joint.

A few months later Lauren's use of alcohol and drugs made

her ill enough to be hospitalized. She refused to go to counseling or workshops and wanted to leave as soon as she felt better. But before she was released hospital staff were able to convince her to go home with her parents.

Like her dismissal from the hospital training program, this was another chance for Lauren to begin self-empowerment—by accepting that drugs were causing her problems. It began well. She didn't drink or use drugs. She found a job and went to church with her parents. But then she met Hal.

Hal went to her parents' church and, from what they saw, he seemed like a nice young man. Lauren liked him, too, in part because he didn't use drugs. She knew little else about him, only that he was divorced. They married and moved to an apartment complex too far south of Chicago for Lauren to keep her new job.

Within a few weeks she lost the progress she had made. She discovered that Hal was sadistic. He tied her to their four-poster bed, held her down at knife point, and burned her with cigarettes. She dreaded his return from work and the look on his face when he came in carrying a wrapped package from the porn store.

"I didn't know how to say no to him and the more I resisted, the meaner he got. My mother had always told me that marriage was for keeps. I tried to convince myself that it was what married people did. I thought there must be something wrong with me. I bought Erica Jong's *The Fear of Flying* and read *The Joy of Sex*. I studied sex manuals and books on how to have a happy mar-

◆ ◆ ◆

riage. I was willing to do anything to keep this marriage going."

Terrified of being abandoned, Lauren returned to smoking pot and using drugs. And the miserable nights and weekends with Hal continued. When she told him she was pregnant he insisted she have an abortion. But Lauren refused. Hal broke her jaw, pushed her down the stairs, and she miscarried.

Lauren began to read books by early feminist writers such as Germaine Greer and Kate Millet. As a result of her reading, she asked Hal if they could move closer to the city so she could go back to work. When he agreed Lauren found another job as a physical therapist.

One Monday morning she arrived at the clinic covered with bruises makeup wouldn't hide. One of the other therapists watching Lauren stuff *Ms.* magazines into her locker said, "He's beating the shit out of you, isn't he?" Lauren gasped and whispered, "I thought no one knew." The colleague put her arm around Lauren. "I know a counselor you could see."

Lauren went to the counselor, who told her that until she liked herself more she would settle for any kind of treatment, even abuse. Lauren felt enough confidence to go home and tell Hal that if he ever hit her again, he would have to leave. Hal meekly promised to stop.

But the next week he beat her again. Lauren threw his clothes and fishing poles out the window and told him to get out. She filed for divorce.

Here again was another critical moment that might have led Lauren to accepting. She seemed able to acknowledge that she had a problem—but she thought it was Hal.

♦ ♦ ♦

And for a brief time she responded to others' support, but then retreated from the counselor and her friends, gave up her job, and lived alone.

Not yet realizing that her problem was drugs or knowing that she was drawn to men likely to be uncaring and cruel, Lauren began going out with Bob. When Bob moved in with her he brought along his companions, all heavy drug users who robbed trucks for a living.

"Bobby gave me my first taste of heroin. It wiped out my need for anything else."

When Bob was caught stealing from trucks during the blizzard of '78, he and Lauren fled to Tampa, Florida. They moved into a rooming house in the drug traffic area where they could buy anything they wanted, day or night. Most days Lauren was oblivious to her surroundings and refused her parents' phone calls.

Within a year she was hospitalized for cirrhosis of the liver, hepatitis, and pneumonia. On her release she was given a welfare check intended for food, but she and Bob used the money for drugs. When their drugs were gone, Bob shoved her out the door and told her not to come back without cash.

Too sick and weak to argue, on the nights they needed money for drugs, Lauren walked the streets. She looked for men to pick her up and turned tricks in their cars.

"One night I was out of dope and out of money. I was walking slowly along the sidewalk when a van stopped. I thought it was someone I had tricked with. But as soon as I got in the driver said, 'You're under arrest.' "

When Bob heard the news he ran off to his mother's apartment in Chicago. Sentenced to six months in jail, Lauren lived

◆ ◆ ◆

with twenty-five cellmates. Without drugs she suffered agonizing withdrawal symptoms, threatened suicide, and was moved into solitary confinement.

Four months later Lauren walked out the metal door of the jailhouse. She had withdrawn from drugs. She had come close to dying more than once. She stood on the street in the warm Florida sun holding a small vinyl overnight bag, trying to decide where to go.

The decision she made ultimately led to her moment of truth. Lauren stepped out into the street and began hitching rides to Chicago. She moved in with Bob and found a job in a factory, putting boxes together. She drank beer for breakfast, smoked joints at lunch, and drank after dinner until she fell asleep.

Two months later she and Bob had a fight, and he stabbed her with a kitchen knife. The police drove Bob to jail and Lauren to a hospital. Her parents rushed to see her and pleaded with her to try the hospital's drug treatment program. Lauren agreed, but after the first session she wanted to quit.

"They talked about losses and I didn't want to hear it. Sure, I'd lost a few things, but so what. I could blame every loss on something or someone else. And I didn't think I could live without ever drinking again."

Because she had entered the program for her parents—not for herself—she dropped out. With no place to go, Lauren took her few remaining possessions to the train station and stored them in a locker.

"I didn't know what to do. But then I ran into a friend

• • •

downtown and moved into her apartment. She was hooking. I didn't want to get into that, but I had to do a couple tricks to get some money."

Lauren's friend told her about a man she saw every week on Michigan Avenue and offered the job to Lauren. "It'll be a hundred for you," she said, and held out a piece of paper with his address. Lauren took it and dressed in skintight jeans, a black tube top, and red four-inch heels.

Early the next morning, when she walked out of the man's condominium, two men grabbed her in an attempt to steal her purse. While she was yelling and fighting them off, the police heard the scuffle and picked her up. They dropped her off at a shelter for the homeless. Lauren fell asleep on a bench in the waiting room.

The next day the sun shining through the windows wakened Lauren. She felt so miserable she wished she could die. At six A.M. the shelter opened and the day staff arrived. Fay, an older woman with a pleasant, weathered face, saw Lauren lying on the bench. She put a sweet roll and a cup of warm coffee on a small plastic tray and walked toward her. Lauren shielded her eyes, not sure where she was, and tried to sit up.

"You're in pretty rough shape," Fay said. "Why don't you stay a few days?"

Lauren looked down at her "happy hooker outfit." She lay back on the bench and moaned. "I've got to," she thought. "I've got no more fight."

Fay pulled a stool over near the bench and sat down. She

♦ ♦ ♦

put her hand on Lauren's shoulder and Lauren thought how nonjudgmental Fay was.

"I know what you're going through," Fay said. "I'm a recovering addict. You'll feel better in a few days."

Lauren sat up again, looked at the other street people sleeping in the shelter, and felt horrified. She wondered what she had gotten herself into. She lay back down and began to tremble.

Fay got out a blanket and laid it over Lauren. "Do you want to go to a detox?" Fay asked, as she tucked the blanket tightly around Lauren.

Lauren thought about Fay's question. She had no where else to go and finally said, "I'm scared."

"We all are, every day, for some reason," Fay said.

Lauren stood up slowly, letting the blanket slide to the floor. "I've got to get my bag. It's at the train station," she said.

"Will you come back?" Fay asked, picking up the blanket and folding it into a square.

"Yes," Lauren said, and rushed out the door.

Fay waved good-bye, but she felt weary. She'd heard stories about bags in train stations before.

As Lauren walked along the street in downtown Chicago she felt conspicuous—a night person out among the day people. She wished she'd gone earlier so she wouldn't have to pass men and women in suits and dresses on their way to work. To avoid them, she ducked into an alley. Several men she recognized were putting together change to buy a bottle and asked Lauren to join them. She thought about it. But to escape she said she had somewhere to go and might return that night.

♦ ♦ ♦

Lauren's hands shook. She thought she'd feel better if she had a drink. She saw a liquor store a few blocks ahead and when she got to the door she couldn't stop herself from walking in. She asked for a nip bottle of vodka and tucked it into a pocket.

Outside in the sunlight, she hurried to the train station, found her locker, and recovered her bag. Remembering Fay's compassion, she quickly dropped the bottle into a trash bin and ran all the way back to the shelter.

"Oh, you came back," Fay said, and smiled.

If Lauren was ready to change, by admitting that she was a drug addict who needed help, why had accepting been so elusive to her? Why did she have to suffer to the point of hitting bottom before she could face her problem and feel responsibility for the person she'd become?

To answer these questions it may help to reflect back on Donna's situation and recall the love and validation she received from her family. Donna's family had affirmed her, enabling her to feel love and confidence in herself, resulting in high self-value. Because she considered herself worthy and valuable, she was able to look out for herself, no matter how painful or frustrating her circumstances.

Not everyone has a background that fosters self-confidence. Not every child grows up knowing love and affirmation. If young people are treated poorly, over time they internalize that information and come to view themselves the way others see them, or the way they think others see them.

Lauren had always wondered about her biological parents but was afraid questions would upset her adoptive parents.

♦ ♦ ♦

Because she didn't ask, she acquired the notion that her natural parents didn't want her and that her adoptive parents might not, as well. Her assumption that she wasn't lovable formed the basis for low self-value. No matter how much her adoptive parents protected her, or maybe because they protected her too much, Lauren thought she was unworthy.

Even though her parents were responsible people who tried to give her everything they thought a child could want, they were unable to provide her with the assurance and affection she craved. Their emotional distance increased her insecurity and self-doubt.

Lauren turned to her grandmother for affirmation and unconditional love. After her grandmother died, she was overcome by fears of being abandoned. When she couldn't get from her parents the closeness she'd known with her grandmother, she felt an even greater loss and emptiness.

Her view of her father as indifferent led her to seek out emotionally unavailable men who would mistreat her in some way. Janet Woititz describes this dynamic in *The Struggle for Intimacy:* "The challenge to win the love of an erratic and sometimes rejecting person repeats the challenge of your childhood. You are grateful when the inconsistent person throws you a crumb, but get bored quickly with the one who is available all the time." When Lauren picked out men like her father she was on an unconscious level still trying to get her father's love. If she could win the love of an emotionally distant man, she thought that would prove she was lovable. Failing to get such reassurance further reduced her self-value. And, in a vicious circle, her low self-value kept her in these destructive relationships, and those relationships kept her self-value low.

♦ ♦ ♦

Lauren was plagued by insecurities. It is easy to understand her susceptibility to drugs, her desire to escape her reality. And more than likely she carried a genetic predisposition toward addiction, inherited from one or both of her birth parents.

With addiction came denial—part of the disease—and Lauren readily fell into denying what was happening. She denied that drugs caused her problems in school and in relationships. She rationalized her drug-affected behavior, Hal's sadistic demands, and Bobby's insistence that she become a prostitute—anything to justify using drugs.

"Addiction, or compulsivity, is a pathological relationship with a mood-altering event, experience, or thing that has life-damaging consequences. Addicts are driven by a force outside themselves; they believe that happiness lies in something other than the self," John Bradshaw writes in the March '89 issue of *Lears.*

Lauren's addiction and preoccupation with avoiding reality kept her sense of inferiority high and her self-value low. Not caring about herself, she couldn't help herself or let others help her—until she met Fay.

Seeing herself through Fay's eyes was like looking, for the first time, at what she had become. In those first tender moments with Fay at the shelter she'd realized, with terror, what her reality was. Somewhere inside, Lauren unearthed a seed of self-value—planted by her grandmother and tended by her parents' unfailing concern—that enabled her, at last, to begin to look at and care for herself.

Being willing to see problems—as they are—is essential to handling them. Problems, of course, are of many kinds and vary in degree of severity. First there are the ones that seem to come about through no fault of our own, such as accidents, illnesses, physical disabilities, abuse, fears, phobias, and the death of loved ones. Then there are the problems we feel we bring upon ourselves through negligence or lack of self-discipline. These are the problems we feel most responsible for and find the ones most difficult to acknowledge.

And when we deny what is happening we lose not only our reality but also our options. Not until we can admit the truth to ourselves can change become a possibility.

When avoiding and denying we may con ourselves into thinking we're escaping our problems. Drifting may forestall the moment of truth, but it will ultimately come. By the time it does we may have accumulated far more serious consequences to confront.

And when the inevitable confrontation comes, what do we do? We may begin by answering such questions as: What is happening? What has happened to me? Is there anything I can do about it? How am I contributing to this situation?

Awareness leads to acceptance, as it did for Lauren, and she then made a decision to get well. In *The Courage to Heal,* Bass and Davis describe this moment. "Deciding to heal, making your own growth and recovery a priority, sets in motion a healing force that will bring to your life a richness and depth you never dreamed possible."

With Lauren's acceptance and decision came an openness to others' offers of help. She became active in the search to find the support she would need and began networking right away.

◆ ◆ ◆

That night Lauren visited the city detoxification unit. She sat in a large room listening to people tell how they'd become addicted, what happened to them, and how they recovered. She was particularly attentive when an attractive young woman got up to speak. The woman had gone to private schools and had started drinking in college. She turned to prostitution to support a drug habit and had spent time in jail. Drugs and prostitution behind her, she was now working as a photographer for a newspaper.

Lauren couldn't believe what she was hearing. She felt as if she and the speaker were the only ones in the room. She began to cry. And when the session was over, she went up to the woman.

"I know you were telling *your* story," Lauren said, "but it was *my* life." Lauren covered her eyes with her hands.

"That's okay," the former prostitute said and put her arm around Lauren. "Let it out, honey."

"It's so strange; it's almost scary to find out somebody else has been there, too. I thought I was alone, the only one."

"You're not alone anymore." The woman wrote down her phone number and gave it to Lauren. "Call me anytime," she said. "And I'll see you next week."

Before she began the second stage, networking, Lauren thought she had a defective character, that she was a worthless person. She didn't know that she had a disease that caused destructive, degrading behavior. It was reassuring to hear from others like Fay and the exhooker that she had al-

◆ ◆ ◆

coholism. It couldn't be cured, but it could be arrested. As she came to believe that she was not bad, weak, or immoral, she began to feel better about herself.

In the beginning Fay and the exhooker were Lauren's strongest supporters, her empowering examples. She spent hours talking to each of them and their caring helped Lauren learn to care for herself. As she responded to their encouragement, her self-value improved.

In *The Courage to Heal,* Bass and Davis recommend getting support from other survivors. "It's unlikely that anyone other than another survivor can listen as much as you'll need to talk. . . . Change requires support and community. If you do not get it from the people closest to you, seek it elsewhere, whether through new friends, a counselor, or a group of other survivors. . . . Being with someone actively engaged in the healing process means that you are in a growing relationship, not a stagnant one."

Staying with that support, continuing those relationships, will make the difference between long- and short-term success. For example, when a fellow therapist noticed Lauren's bruises and offered compassion and the name of a counselor, Lauren responded briefly. She took some steps to help herself: she saw the counselor and managed to get Hal out of her life. But rather than continue to be supported, she stopped seeing the counselor, her friends, and working. When she deprived herself of support, she regressed to self-destructive behavior and debilitating relationships.

But as Lauren progressed through the stages of self-empowerment she wanted to stay close to her network of support. She needed the assurance of knowing that others cared about her and understood her. Her network of support became her means of building self-value. The caring, concern, and affirmation of other people helped her to raise her level of self-value. When her self-value improved, change would then be possible, options would be open to her.

As Lauren's self-value increased she began to feel responsible for her circumstances. And from there she was able to recognize choices and make difficult decisions.

Lauren asked the staff at the city detox to find her a safe place to live, away from any temptation to use drugs. She was relieved when her counselor found a residential treatment facility for women on the outskirts of the city, but she became nervous when she heard she could not be admitted until she'd met the director.

The day before her interview Lauren colored her hair with an auburn rinse. She rummaged through boxes of old clothes at the detox and picked out a green polyester pant suit, too large, and a plastic purse that matched. On the day of the interview she stood in front of a full-length mirror. She hated the way she looked, head-to-toe polyester, still bloated and bulgy. Her parents drove her to the center.

"I was so scared. The walk up those steps was the longest walk. It helped to look up and see the director waiting for me. She was tan and had on a sharp black and white suit with a white silk blouse. She was beautiful. I looked down at myself in borrowed clothes, fat and ugly. I was nothing."

Lauren and the director went inside, where it was quiet because residents were in group sessions. Lauren sat down in front of the director's desk.

♦ ♦ ♦

"Lauren, you can call me Mary. I'm a recovering addict and alcoholic, and I want you to have a chance to start over."

"Thank you," Lauren said softly. She couldn't picture Mary with a drinking or a drug problem.

"We have rules here," Mary said. "After you've been here six weeks, you'll have to get a job to pay for your board and room."

Lauren nodded. She could hear women's voices and laughter coming from the living room.

"You'll have to do chores to help keep the house clean."

"I'm willing to do anything," Lauren said.

"But, and this is important, do you want to stop drinking?" Mary looked into Lauren's brown eyes.

"Yes. I want what you have. I've been missing life and doing everything to block it out. I haven't seen anything but my own existence and I don't want to look at that. I want my life back."

When the interview was over Lauren returned to the detox to wait. A few days later her application for admission was accepted, but a bed would not be available for four weeks. Lauren didn't think she could wait that long or that the city detox would let her stay another month. And she didn't trust herself to live alone or with her parents.

"Waiting was the hardest part. I needed constant reassurance from the staff at the detox that they wouldn't turn me out until I could get into the center, and they didn't."

A month later Lauren moved into the treatment center. "The women living there were so friendly. They were healthy and much more put together than I was. They had something I wanted. Just seeing them so happy without drugs made me

◆ ◆ ◆

want to try. I wanted to get back the good feelings and good times I knew existed. They let me know it was possible."

Lauren found another empowering example in Mary and learned as much as she could from her and the other women. They showed her how different life could be and offered both support and love. She worked hard in workshops, attended recovery group meetings, such as Alcoholics Anonymous and Narcotics Anonymous, and listened to everything she was told.

Lauren had started the third stage, choosing actions that were beneficial. Feeling good about one right choice led her to make the next one. By assuming responsibility for herself she became alert to her chances to choose.

For the past several years she'd had no idea that she had choices or that change for her was even a possibility. She'd been enslaved by addiction, victimized by men who mistreated her, and was unable to see any other course but a downhill one. Suddenly she was exhilarated by the discovery that she had choices.

Like Lauren, we, too, have choices—about our attitude and our approach to circumstances. How we choose to look at our problems affects how we handle them.

What happens to us is not nearly as important as what we believe has happened. If we tell ourselves someone else is to blame for our predicament, we stay stuck and we can't go forward. If we cling to resentments, we give up our power to change, and we also give ourselves permission to fail. But if we can look at our situations in a new way—such as feeling gratitude for an opportunity to master the challenge in front of us and for the chance to start again—we might see our chances to choose.

And with the recognition that there are chances to choose, we can decide to act on them or not. We have control over what we will do, even if it sometimes seems like two steps forward and one step backward.

"No choice, no decision we make, will be wrong" the anonymous author of *Each Day a New Beginning* writes. "A particular decision may lead us slightly astray, down a dead-end path, perhaps—but we can always turn back and choose again . . . no choice is all-powerful regarding our destiny. We are offered chances again and again for making the right choices, the ones that will most contribute to the bigger plan for our lives."

Lauren had a bigger plan for herself. The idea of life on the streets had become unthinkable. She wanted much more for herself and came to believe she deserved it. In the process of choosing actions that would take her to her goals, she approached a positive shift. One of her choices was to learn as much as she could about addiction.

"I learned that this disease was spiritual, mental, and physical. Spiritual because it destroyed my values, mental because I was obsessed with drugs, and physical because of my craving for more—once I'd started. They told us to forgive ourselves and the people who had enabled us to drink.

"I found out that I'd probably inherited this disease from my biological parents. Alcoholism runs in families, either caused by a genetic predisposition, environmental factors, or

♦ ♦ ♦

both. Children of alcoholics are more likely than others to become alcoholics, even if they are adopted by people who don't have a problem.

"I began to understand my adoptive parents better. They couldn't help the way they were. In fact, they'd both come from alcoholic homes, but their families had kept it secret. So they didn't know they were adult children of alcoholics. They didn't drink, but they hadn't had any treatment. Without counseling, they had the characteristics of those raised in dysfunctional families and that affected me."

What Lauren was learning is explained by Sharon Wegscheider in *Another Chance: Hope and Health for the Alcoholic Family*. "All chemically dependent people, alcoholics (or others) suffer from very low self-worth. As a result they are incapable of either maintaining a healthy marriage relationship or encouraging children to develop high self-worth. Soon, each family member's growing sense of worthlessness feeds on every other member's. Without outside help the entire family will begin to show symptoms of one kind or another. . . ."

"I didn't know that it was hard for my parents," Lauren said, "to have a close relationship with each other or with me. I didn't know why they needed to control me, what I wore and what music I heard. I didn't understand their need to be overly responsible about choosing my friends or schools.

"Living in a household where both parents were perpetuating dyfunctional characteristics, I developed a high tolerance for abnormal behavior. So I didn't consider the ways in which Hal and Bobby treated me to be unusual. I had trouble judging people. I didn't trust my opinions. I doubted myself. I only knew one kind of interaction, and that was dysfunctional.

♦ ♦ ♦

"It helped me to learn these things. I opened up and started to talk about myself in discussion groups and with other women. I really began to like myself.

"I realized that I was basically good and began to think I was entitled to the best there was. And, after a while, I knew I could have it.

"I discovered the joyous person in me. For the first time in years I could see the different shades of green in summer. It was all brand new."

Lauren had entered the fourth stage, shifting. She had no doubt about what she wanted for herself and no uncertainty about going after it. Her commitment to herself was working. She was starting to feel the benefits of her choices and enjoying the results.

Just as Lauren held up a new image of who she was, we, too, when we come the fourth stage of self-empowerment, will have a new vision for ourselves. It may be a thinner version of ourselves, a more independent version of ourselves, or a stronger, healthier version of ourselves. But it is our vision. And no matter what that vision is, we begin experiencing the joy of it. That joy keeps us going.

"Personal creativity is a continuous process of bringing forth a changing vision of oneself, and of oneself in relation to the world," Jean Baker Miller writes in *Toward a New Psychology of Women.* "Out of this creation each person determines her/his next step and is motivated to take that next step."

At this point in self-empowerment taking the next steps and making the right choices come much more easily. A commitment to the new vision helps us to get past ever-present temptations to relapse, revert, or regress.

After four weeks Mary reminded Lauren that it was time to find a job. On her way to an interview with a doctor in Chicago, Lauren was stopped on the sidewalk by a man she recognized. He had been a pusher.

"Hey, babe, I missed ya," he said. "I just got out. Did three years. Where's everyone?" Lauren tried to keep on walking; she didn't want to talk to him.

He followed her, grabbed her sleeve, and asked again, "Hey, where's everybody?"

"I don't know," Lauren said. She brushed him away and hurried toward the doctor's office. Happy that the doctor hired her, she returned quickly to the house. She was relieved to see Mary and her new friends again.

A week later Lauren's intentions were tested again. At one of her recovery group meetings she met a young man who had been sober three years. She'd been warned not to get involved with anyone until she'd been sober a year.

"Emery was tall and handsome and wonderful. When we met something just clicked and we fell in love. We couldn't stay away from each other. We checked into the same motel every weekend. And on Mondays I had a smile from ear to ear."

When Lauren grew concerned about doing anything that would endanger her sobriety, she decided to wait until she'd completed her program at the center before making a big decision about Emery. Through his caring and the new way of life she was learning at the center, she came to appreciate all that her adoptive parents had done for her, especially their unconditional love.

Lauren was touched when Emery formally asked her father's permission to marry. Her mother arranged a small wedding in their church and the day after Christmas they were married.

That spring Lauren considered changing her career. She was interested in women. She knew from her own experiences how badly they could be used and abused. She thought she could help women, perhaps even defend them. She had a vision for herself as a women's advocate, but knew that meant more college courses and law school. The next September she enrolled in college for prelaw courses.

On campus Lauren noticed many students using drugs and remembered how her own drug problem began her freshman year. She wanted to help students learn more about drugs by setting up an information center where they could ask questions. She designed a flyer. Her mother made copies and helped with distribution. Lauren staffed the center and when it grew too big to run herself she enlisted help from students who had overcome drug problems.

Lauren then saw a need to educate doctors about student use of drugs and alcohol. She created a series of "Drug Awareness" seminars for professionals in Chicago's educational and medical communities. Her mother printed, addressed, and mailed the invitations. Lauren introduced the speakers and often told some of her own story.

Even before entering law school she had become a role model and an empowering example for others, especially young women. She knew that she could make a difference, particularly when she shared what had happened to her.

◆ ◆ ◆

Lauren moved naturally into mentoring, the final stage of self-empowerment. She knew she was a survivor, but she didn't know that taking on a survivor mission—to help others avoid drug problems—would also be helping herself. She came to it instinctively.

By becoming an empowering example, she was reinforcing her own achievements. Because students looked up to her and counted on her example, she couldn't let them down. She wouldn't be lured by any temptation to slide backward into previous ways of thinking or acting. She wanted to continue going forward. Becoming a role model for others ensured that.

"Now that I have my life back," Lauren said in our final interview, "I want to live it to the fullest. I enjoy feeling again and thinking clearly. I think of using chemicals as not living. I have so much to lose if I go back to heroin and hooking. And I don't mean material things; I mean myself, my self-esteem.

"I know I am a woman with a great deal to contribute. After what I've been through I feel I can go after anything. And I'm not afraid to."

KIM

♦ ♦ ♦

"I don't want anyone, especially a homeless mother, to ever feel it's too late to change."

4

Before visiting Kim I was told not to carry a camera, so I wouldn't be mistaken for a reporter, and to look as inconspicuous as possible. Kim was living in a welfare hotel for homeless women and their families in New York City. She was thirty-five, the mother of twelve children. Kim hadn't always been homeless. She had gone to college, married, worked, and bought a house. She had supported her children, then a husband, and later a boyfriend.

At the hotel Kim had become a role model for homeless

♦ ♦ ♦

women and, as their spokesperson, received considerable media attention. For the past two years she had worked to get herself and many other women at the hotel off welfare. She had fought against the use of drugs, prevalent in the hotel, started a newspaper, and organized the Hotel Tenant Rights Project.

Even though I had dressed simply, when I walked through the Forty-second Street entrance uniformed security guards holding walkie-talkies to their ears closed in around me. Did I have a photo ID? Who was I seeing? How long was I staying? I was told to go no farther and to speak through an iron grate to the guard seated behind it.

While the guard behind the grate made calls and wrote on a pad between glances at me, I looked around the lobby. There were vestiges of a once elegant hotel. A black and white marble tiled floor showed beneath a thin layer of cigarette butts. Regal pilasters and intricately carved wood were visible behind institution-green paint, curling in loose flaps. Walls that I imagined had once been backdrops for tapestries and paintings were now host to graffiti, meeting notices, and "crack pot" posters with hotline numbers.

That morning the lobby teemed with women talking to each other, most of them women of color, wearing jeans, denim jackets, and sneakers. Many of them were pregnant, jiggling carriages or cloth strollers, holding a baby and watching young children at the same time. At the other end of the lobby another congregation of women and children waited patiently in front of two small, chrome elevator doors.

A guard clutching an orange plastic milk crate ushered me past the lobby elevators to a cagelike freight elevator in the back of the hotel. Carrying its stench of urine, stale cigarettes,

♦ ♦ ♦

and spoiling food, the elevator lurched up and swung precariously. I was relieved when it finally arrived at the eleventh floor and I could get out.

The guard knocked on a door and a smiling black woman, holding a baby, answered. Over a full figure Kim wore jeans, a T-shirt, and a denim jacket. She was gracious, yet reserved. The guard watched us closely, then sat down on his crate outside the door. "You're gonna have to sit there a long time," she said to him, "because this lady's gonna be here all day."

At first I felt nonchalant about the guards, thinking the tight security was to keep conditions at the hotel under wraps. But later I wondered if the guards might also be protecting me.

Inside the eight-by-ten-foot room Kim was warm and friendly. There was a metal double bunk, a cot, two dressers, and a waist-high refrigerator. She showed me where a hot plate was hidden underneath the cot. The top shelf of the clothes closet held a row of cheese curls, pretzels, cereal, potato chips, and crackers. Another open door led to a bathroom, shared with tenants in the next room.

Kim had borrowed this room for our interview while its tenant went to Kim's three rooms to take care of her preschool children. After talking for several hours, we went to Kim's rooms when her school-age children were home. She wanted me to see all twelve children and a seven-month-old grandchild, too.

Kim was raising a family as large as the one she had grown up in, but she thought she could avoid repeating her mother's problems. The tenth of thirteen children, Kim had seen her father beat her mother and her mother give way to a nervous breakdown. She had watched with fear and sadness as eight older brothers and sisters were taken away and placed in foster homes or put up for adoption.

Kim was five years old when she held her younger sister's hand and walked up the steps into her first foster home, in North Philadelphia. She liked the large house because it had a yard with apple trees. Ms. Butler, a black woman with gray hair worn in a bun, who had raised thirty-five foster children and recently received an award for her work, showed Kim her room.

Even though Kim's older sisters, Cynthia and Geneva, were already there, Kim cried and begged to go back home. A few days later she felt more comfortable but sensed that Ms. Butler's daughters didn't want her there.

Kim tried to make friends with her older sisters, whom she had never really known. She thought Geneva was loving but not Cynthia. "Cynthia was color conscious. Because she was light-skinned, she thought she was beautiful. I was dark-skinned, got left out of things, and didn't think I could be popular.

"But Ms. Butler taught me to love myself. She taught me to respect all races of people and that black was just as beautiful as light or white. She gave me confidence. She loved me. I never heard the word foster mother. I called her Grandma.

"Grandma told me to love my mother. She explained that my mother had had a hard life and two bad marriages and she couldn't take care of us the way she wanted. She said that it took a good woman to say she couldn't handle it and that my mother wanted us to have the best. She told me to never feel ashamed of what happened to me. She said it was not my

♦ ♦ ♦

fault. She said I had a good mother and I should be proud of her."

Many years before, Ms. Butler's husband had left her with three small children. She was an uneducated woman who couldn't read past a third-grade level. To make money and still be home to raise her children, she had gone into foster care. She kept her house spotlessly clean and cooked good meals. She taught Kim to sew, clean, and crochet. Kim crocheted the strings for all the lights in the house. Grandma also showed her correct table manners, how to walk, how to dress, how to approach people—and encouraged her to try hard at school.

In third grade Kim was placed in special education classes because her speech was not clear and also, she thinks now, because of a belief that children from broken or foster homes had something wrong with them. Yet her marks were excellent. Grandma requested another evaluation and, in sixth grade, Kim was put into a regular classroom.

Kim was thirteen when she had a fight with one of Ms. Butler's daughters. The daughter accused Kim of taking her mother's love and wanted to know what was wrong with Kim's mother that she didn't take care of Kim herself.

After the fight Grandma hugged Kim and lovingly reassured and comforted her. Kim felt sad because she knew how heartbreaking such an argument was to Grandma. The next morning when Grandma didn't get up at six, as she usually did, Kim was worried. She waited awhile and then went into her room. She found her beloved Ms. Butler dead. She'd had a heart attack.

◆ ◆ ◆

Accepting the death of this remarkable woman, who during eight years had influenced her life more than anyone else, was one of the hardest things Kim ever had to do. Just as difficult was accepting that she was now entirely responsible for herself. At thirteen she juggled feelings of overwhelming loss with fears about her future. She didn't know who would care for her or her sisters, or where they would live.

"We adapt, with enormous difficulty," Judith Viorst writes in *Necessary Losses,* "to the altered circumstances of our life, modifying—in order to survive—our behavior, our expectations, our self-definitions."

Kim would now have to adjust her expectations and challenge her self-definition—one that Grandma had helped her to form. Grandma had taken in a homeless, dark-skinned child and cherished her. That flow of unconditional love had fostered in a bewildered youngster a sense of healthy self-love. And further, by showing respect to Kim's mother, Grandma had helped Kim to respect herself. Grandma had instilled confidence in Kim and taught her to believe that she was a beautiful person. Grandma had left Kim with a lifetime legacy, the gift of high self-value, that would help her cope with her present and future trials.

Like Donna, Kim's high self-value was the result of validation in childhood—an interesting phenomenon because their two childhoods were so different. Donna had known family life as fun, happy, secure, and loving. Kim hadn't known a normal family life: she didn't know where most of her brothers and sisters were; she didn't have a consistent relationship with

♦ ♦ ♦

her mother; and she didn't know her father at all. But because of Ms. Butler's nurturing, she considered herself fortunate and thought that her childhood had been a good one.

A healthy self-value doesn't depend on social status or a combination of ideal circumstances. Self-value doesn't result from money, education, or other forms of security. Rather, self-value comes from the people around us. It is reflected in their faces and voices. It comes from being affirmed, loved, and valued. We absorb those reflections and make them part of our self-image.

Not everyone has a Ms. Butler to help them form such a good self-image. Although it may not be readily apparent, most people have, however, received validation from someone. If not from parents, there may have been a loving grandparent, a kind neighbor, or an interested teacher.

Consider the people who have an impact today—which relationships are energizing, which are enervating? Who usually encourages and supports us? Who doesn't? Are there relationships we should let go of? Or people we could invite into our life whose love would help build our self-image?

A reasonably high level of self-value is a prerequisite for change. It is essential for self-empowerment, essential for growth. "When we grow," Scott Peck writes in *The Road Less Traveled,* "it is because we are working at it, and we are working at it because we love ourselves." If a sense of self-love still feels elusive, that can be worked on in the next stage, networking.

For now the focus is on identifying the current situation that most needs attention. This can be done not only by acknowledging and saying out loud exactly what the problem is, but also by deciding to take responsibility for it and oneself.

♦ ♦ ♦

Each woman in this book begins to work on her problem at the moment when she comes to terms with it and accepts it. Kim's problem was finding herself alone as a young teen and having to become responsible for herself and her younger sister Linda. But with the legacy from Ms. Butler, she knew instinctively she would need other people. As her story continues, notice when she asks for help, when she continues or ends relationships, and how she uses networking to achieve positive change.

For the next few years Kim lived in a series of foster homes. First she and Linda moved in with a West Indian woman. They liked her but were terrified by her boyfriend, who got drunk, was "fresh" with them, and tried to lure them into his bed or onto the couch with fifty-dollar bills.

When the woman married her boyfriend she moved out and left Kim and Linda, unsupervised, alone in her house. Because Grandma had taught them to cook and clean, they were able to look out for themselves for a while. Out of the welfare money their absentee foster mother received for the girls' care, she gave them seven dollars a week for food and public transportation to school. They couldn't manage on that and Kim dropped out of school.

Kim initiated a search for their natural mother, found her, and asked her to live with them in the second foster mother's house. The welfare agency returned the girls to their mother's care and provided public assistance funds for their support.

"But we found out that our mother was not a well woman. She had a bad temper. She didn't have the patience to raise us. She had a drinking problem and sometimes got so mad

♦ ♦ ♦

she hit us with bottles, with anything. I had to hold her hands together to keep her from hitting us. Sometimes I was so scared, I had to take Linda and run away for the night."

That year Kim met Sam, who was two years older than her fifteen years. They played hookie together, often spending whole days at his house. "My mother didn't like the idea of me having a boyfriend. Her heart had gotten hard after two bad marriages. Men were no good, she said. She wanted God to put them all in an everlasting fire with the devil.

"That time of my life with my real mother was very sad, and I felt very alone. When my mother couldn't cope any more and left, we had to find somewhere else to live."

Kim's third foster mother was a woman in West Philadelphia, whom Kim admired for the elegant way she dressed, her beautiful house, and her devotion to religion. But the woman expected Kim to scrub the rugs on her hands and knees, clean the bathrooms, and do what was called "the low work." Although Kim had her own room and bath, she had to sleep in the woman's room—to fetch books and slippers. "She was so controlling and I felt like I was bowing down to her. I didn't want to stay there anymore."

Kim went to live with her older sister Cynthia, who had become a buyer for a department store. During the year she lived with her sister, Kim received her high school equivalency diploma and enrolled in a city-funded college program.

She was still seeing Sam and, at nineteen, became pregnant. When Cynthia insisted that Kim have an abortion, she refused. Kim didn't believe in abortion and wanted to have Sam's baby. Because Sam didn't want to get married, Kim moved in with a girlfriend. When her first baby, Louis, was born, Sam's mother took care of him so Kim could complete her college work. A year later she and Sam had another baby, Keisha. Kim thought Sam gambled and drank too much, decided she saw no future with him, and ended their relationship.

She started seeing Mike, a handsome man who'd had many girlfriends. He praised her steadiness and determination to make something of herself. She was twenty-two, pregnant, and had two babies when she married Mike. They moved into public housing. Kim worked for the welfare department and raised the children. She had tried various forms of birth control, but because of side effects and because she didn't like them, she preferred not to use them.

Pregnant with her fourth child, Kim needed help and asked her natural mother, who'd been treated for alcoholism, to come back and live with her. Kim's mother, who'd trained as a nurse's aide, watched Kim also become a nurse's aide. But then she urged her daughter to get certified in public health nursing. Kim went back to school while her mother took care of her grandchildren.

For long periods of time Kim's husband was gone. When he did come home, they argued. Her mother was supportive of Kim and spared no words with Mike. She told Mike he was lousy for being away so much, that he was heading nowhere, that her daughter didn't need any more babies, and that she could make it on her own.

Kim got a job in a home for retarded children, but felt it left her with no energy for her own children. She went to work for an abortion clinic, but couldn't stay because she didn't believe in abortion. She finally found a job she loved, working in a maternity ward.

◆ ◆ ◆

"I was on the job one day when a new mother died. I cried for the patient, but I knew I was also crying for myself. I just couldn't hold myself together any longer."

Kim's supervisor sat down next to her. She asked what was wrong. Kim needed to talk. "My marriage is breaking up," she said. "I found out my husband is also a gambler. He is saying he doesn't know what I am trying to prove by going to college. My independence threatens him."

The supervisor encouraged Kim to talk out her feelings. Kim also found another older woman she could talk to. "She helped me, too. I didn't realize other women were having the same problems I was."

When Kim began networking she was combining dependence on herself with a healthy dependence on others to help her do what she wanted and needed. As she found new people to empower her, she never forgot her first empowering example. Ms. Butler had shown Kim by her example that a woman could cope with unexpected problems, such as being a single mother. And by raising Kim to have an unwavering view of herself, Ms. Butler had prepared Kim to handle whatever happened to her and to welcome offers of help.

Kim learned from her sister's example of professional success and benefitted from her mother's encouragement to go further with her career. Kim was also empowered by her supervisor's compassion and the older woman's wisdom.

We, too, may be exposed to people who can help us, but their guidance won't have any effect unless we care about ourselves first. Advice and suggestions—no matter how appropriate—will go unheeded until we've acquired a good level of self-value.

When we feel we are at a point where help is available, but we can't make use of it to cope, change, or grow, this networking stage can be used to raise our level of self-value. Rather than seek guidance for a specific situation, we'll first want to get support. We can ask one or two family members or friends for their encouragement and caring, so we can learn to care about ourselves. We may feel a need to reach out beyond our immediate circle for someone with a similar problem, especially one who has mastered it. At the same time we can look for a support group and try to connect with people capable of affirming us.

Once we've found support we can talk openly, explaining what we need, what we want to do, even that we need to value ourselves. Perhaps we have memories that don't contribute much to our self-value. We may feel embarrassed, ashamed. It will help to talk about these things. Our support people, more than likely, will consider these confessions of what we think is abhorrent behavior to be much more normal and far less dreadful than we do. They can assure us that our behavior was either understandable, acceptable, or forgiveable. This can bring relief and peace.

In time, with this kind of support, we sense a difference in our view of ourselves. We start to believe in our abilities. We care enough about ourselves to make use of offers of help. Then we can begin to go forward and change. This doesn't mean, of course, that suddenly everything will be magical or that we'll always be strong or consistently make the right choices, but networking for support to raise our self-value is the place to begin.

♦ ♦ ♦

"Feeling occasionally inadequate and uncertain about one's own value . . . may be inevitable . . . and it may be healthy," Sanford and Donovan write in *Women and Self-Esteem.* "Yet there's a difference between occasionally doubting and always being uncertain, and there's nothing healthy about a woman chronically feeling she isn't 'worth it.' High self-esteem doesn't protect us from self-doubts, but it does enable us to entertain self-doubt without being devastated."

Although Kim felt self-doubt from time to time, she was never devastated. She was able to continue to look for and respond to support. She began to make one choice after another—some wise, some not, none easy—as she continued through the stages of self-empowerment into choosing.

Kim thought she wanted a divorce and sat down to talk it over with Mike. "No one else will marry you," he said. "You have six kids." But Kim had degrees in social work and nursing and believed she didn't need a husband for support, at least not this husband. "You go on," she said. "I'll pay for the divorce, even if I have to work overtime."

As much as she considered herself capable of independence, Kim was still vulnerable to her first boyfriend's charms. When Sam came back to her, she let him move in. After living with him she realized how much alike Sam and Mike were. Both were jealous, quit jobs, gambled, and drank.

"Sam would never drink in front of the children. That was one good thing about him. And he was fanatical about cleanliness. I appreciated that. He took care of the kids, cooked, and ironed my uniform and the kids' school clothes.

♦ ♦ ♦

"The biggest problem with Sam was work. He wouldn't stay on jobs. He wanted jobs at the top right away and hadn't learned that you have to work for them.

"After several years I decided I didn't want a man just leaning on me. I believed in marriage with an equal partner. I was thirty-two and had to throw Sam out.

"I was by myself, had ten kids, and was pregnant with another. I loved my children, but knew I shouldn't have so many. I didn't like most birth control methods. I had gone into the hospital and had my tubes tied, but something went wrong, and I still got pregnant."

Kim found an abandoned house in West Philadelphia and bought it from the city for twenty-five hundred dollars. The house had no working plumbing, all the pipes had been stolen, and most of the windows were broken. She had the windows fixed and new pipes put in. The repairman told her the heating system would not last and she would need to replace it in about five to six years. Kim began a savings account for the new furnace.

Five years after moving into the house the heating system broke down. Kim had just enough in her savings account to pay for the new furnace.

Just then Sam's mother called Kim and told her Sam was in trouble for borrowing over seven thousand dollars from a loan shark. Sam didn't have the money to repay him. The loan shark and his pals had taken Sam up on a roof, broken his ribs, and slashed his face. They had killed another man who owed them money by pushing him off the roof.

She had six thousand in the bank. Sam was the father of

♦ ♦ ♦

eight of her children. He needed the money as much as she needed the heating system.

"Sam and I made an agreement. I'd pay off his loan and he'd help me get a furnace. Sam's family was there and told him that I was using the stove on the first floor to heat the whole house and that I didn't have to do this. I went with him to North Philadelphia and paid off the loan shark."

The gas company offered to put in Kim's new furnace if a man would cosign the loan. Sam was her common-law husband and she counted on his promise to help get the furnace. "But when it came time to sign, he wouldn't. He resented that he couldn't get in my bed, and to get back at me, he refused to keep his part of our agreement. He called me all types of names and said he wouldn't give me a dime."

Kim sat down with the children to talk over their situation. Without heat she couldn't get anyone to come into the house to care for them. And without a sitter she couldn't go to her job. The children said they hated always feeling so cold and always going to bed wearing coats and boots. Kim promised she would take them to her sister's in New York.

With the older children carrying younger children and wearing backpacks stuffed with clothes, Kim took them on the train to New York. Cynthia's apartment was too small for her three and Kim's eleven children, even for a few days.

Kim was despondent; she never imagined herself following in her mother's footsteps. She thought she could handle having so many children. But she would have to do something and was close to a decision that for her seemed unthinkable.

She went to the child welfare office. Their only solution

was to place her children with foster mothers. Kim couldn't bear being separated from her children or having them separated from each other. She thought it over awhile and then reluctantly agreed, believing it would be only for a short time.

Again she talked to her children. She told them she was going to have to place most of them until she could get matters straightened out. She tried to reassure them, told them she loved them, and that she'd visit often. But they were upset and confused.

The day the social workers arrived in three cars and left with eight of her children, Kim broke down and cried. "Giving them over was the toughest thing I've ever done. I thought I'd never stop crying." She had no idea there'd be trouble getting them back.

"I kept my two oldest, Keisha and Louis, and the youngest, Troy, with me. Most foster homes don't want teenagers. Keisha had just started menstruation, and I felt she had to be with me. Louis was a difficult child, and he needed someone to be patient with him."

Kim, Keisha, Louis, and Troy went to live in a shelter for the homeless. From there they were sent to a motel on Long Island. Then they traveled on the subway from motel to motel, assigned to rooms used by prostitutes during the day that weren't available until late at night.

"We had to wear the same clothes, because when I washed our clothes by hand in a bathroom sink, they didn't dry overnight. On Friday nights I could wash them, because the agency would give us a room for the whole weekend."

After three weeks Kim's social worker got them a room at the welfare hotel. The room was small, but it had its own bathroom. They were relieved to have somewhere to live.

◆ ◆ ◆

Feeling more settled, Kim began the process of getting her other children back. She spoke to one of the managers at the hotel about getting more rooms for her family. "You know I have eight other children that aren't here," she said. He promised that if she could get her kids back, he'd give her the next three rooms that came up.

Kim wrote a letter to the child welfare office requesting the return of her children. Ten days advance notice was required for the return of children who had been placed voluntarily by their mothers. The agency used the time to decide whether to return children to their mothers or to keep them in foster homes.

In Kim's case all of the social workers involved thought her children should be returned to her. But the new supervisor, whose decision it was, disagreed. She thought Kim's housing was inadequate and that the children were better off in homes or given up for adoption.

Kim was so angry she went to see the supervisor. "Have there been any reports against me?" Kim demanded to know. The supervisor said that there hadn't been. "Taking my children is like taking my heart," Kim told her. "I'll have nothing to live for."

When Kim heard that one of the foster mothers wanted to adopt her children, she ran back to the supervisor's office. She was so upset she cursed and threatened to go to court.

At the hotel the manager found three rooms for Kim. He explained that in order to hold them she would need five children sent back right away. Kim made appointments with the new supervisor's supervisor, the assistant director, and the director. All but the new supervisor agreed that the children should go back to Kim.

Finally Kim had to go to court and fight it out. Despite the supervisor's resistance, five children were returned. But the supervisor managed to keep the three youngest.

So the next time Kim went to the agency for a visit with the three youngest she took all of the other children with her. They had a plan. As soon as they arrived they quickly picked up the youngest children and started to walk out.

"Oh, wait a minute!" the staff person said. "You can't take those kids."

"Oh, yes, I can," Kim said. "Watch." Walking close together, they marched out the door, headed for the train, and returned to the hotel.

Kim was choosing every day—whether giving up a marriage that was debilitating, asking Sam to leave, paying off Sam's gambling debt, or kidnapping her own children. When she finally got all her children together at the welfare hotel, she would continue to make choices, some just in order to survive.

Kim had chosen to have many, many children, just as her mother had done. Because a huge family was familiar to Kim and was what she knew, her choice would be called by psychologists a repetition compulsion. Mary Catherine Bates reflects on this idea of repeating the past in *Composing a Life.* "One of the striking facts of most lives is the recurrence of threads of continuity, the reechoing of earlier themes, even across deep rifts of change, but when you watch people damaged by their dependence on continuity, you wonder about

♦ ♦ ♦

the nature of commitment, about the need for a new and more fluid way to imagine the future."

Many of us may see ways in which we repeat the past in our present life. Some of us do it by becoming just like the parent we vowed we'd never emulate, or by choosing a spouse that insures duplication of certain aspects of our parents' marriage. We can also observe in some families such patterns of behavior as addiction, abuse, and battering reappearing generation after generation.

While observing Kim make choices to break patterns, we might recognize that we also are replicating some behavior, learned earlier in our family or from someone else. Are we repeating behavior that we wish we weren't? How can we learn to act, rather than react?

"There are really only two ways to approach life—as victim or as gallant fighter," Merle Shain is quoted in *Each Day a New Beginning,* "and you must decide if you want to act or react, deal your own cards or play with a stacked deck. And if you don't decide which way to play with life, it will always play with you."

In order to deal our own cards, we must become attuned to the times when we have a chance to choose and become conscious of each action associated with the unwanted behavior. Before acting, we may even need to talk to ourselves. What are my choices here? Am I making a decision? Or am I giving up my power to choose? With each conscious choice the unwanted pattern weakens. And then, in the process of changing, we'll be acting—choosing what is best for us—instead of reacting and doing the same things out of habit. We'll be free to choose our friends, our behavior, our lifestyle. We'll become the master of those things we'd been putting up with. At first we may feel strange and uncomfortable. But when rewarded by the results of our new actions, we'll go on to make more and more beneficial choices until we really like this different way of being and acting—and make a committment to it, as Kim did while she was at the welfare hotel.

Kim wanted to work until she discovered that earning money wasn't exactly worthwhile. After she had started a job as a nurse, three days a week on a private case, she learned that most of her salary would be taken for use toward her rent. The welfare department paid twenty-five hundred dollars every two weeks to the hotel's owner for her three small rooms.

And Kim soon realized that she had to be with her children, always alert and ready to protect them. Keisha had been ridiculed for not smoking or drinking and been bitten on the face by another girl. Louis was found unconscious on the floor of the trash room. Another son was injured after being thrown against a cement wall by a drug dealer.

"I had some days when I could've actually killed Sam for getting us into this. I thought of buying a gun. But my kids didn't have anyone but me, so I didn't. Instead I prayed the anger out. I put Sam out of my mind and out of my sight."

For the first few months Kim was at the hotel she was angry. She was outraged by the many injustices she witnessed, such as mothers and children being taken out of their rooms and their door locks plugged because rent checks from welfare to the hotel's owner were late.

When a security guard appeared at her door to lock her and her children out of their rooms, Kim wouldn't submit. She

♦ ♦ ♦

grabbed the guard's walkie-talkie and spoke to the management. "This is Kim—1001, 1002, 1003. I'm not going anywhere and if you plug my door you'd better get ready for a fight." Then she turned to the guard. "Whatever I've got in these rooms, a frying pan or whatever, I'll use it on you." The guard muttered to himself and walked quickly down the hall.

Kim couldn't tolerate the guards' practices. They were allowed to enter the women's rooms whenever they wanted. The guards went out with the women, threatened them, sold them drugs, and hurt their children.

"All of this had to stop. I was very angry seeing these things. Most of the women had come in drug free. But with nothing to do and drugs so available, they got strung out on crack and coke.

"Those rooms really took something out of you. You couldn't put people in those rooms and expect them to come out one hundred percent all right. I just started praying. There were days when I locked my door, didn't want to clean or do anything, and just sat on the bed.

"After a while I knew I couldn't go on the way I was. I told myself that this was better than being on the street. I knew that in some places people were starving. We had food and we had shelter. I didn't have to steal. I didn't have to sell my body.

"So I said to myself that I had to make the best of it, and I had to make changes. Life is what you make it, I told myself. I decided to make it work for me. I decided to make something good happen out of this."

Kim made up her mind not only to leave the hotel but also to do something about conditions there. She told her children they'd get out of the hotel the same way she got them out of the cold house, the same way she got them out of foster homes. She began a search to find a full-time job and a place to live.

Before shifting Kim had been making choices, ranging from withdrawing into depression to battling through the day. On the surface it appeared that she was surviving, but she was merely hanging on. After her shift, however, she stopped lurching from one incident to another and started living on a more stable level. Her anger turned to energy. Chaos and confusion reemerged as serenity.

In the process of reaching this shift, Kim's focus had changed. Through prayer she let go of some of her anger. She turned her raging resentment against Sam into a commitment to help herself, her children, and other mothers. Her commitment created a vision; her vision guided her actions. She knew what she was going to do; not what she'd like to do or wanted to do but what she was going to do.

Making a positive shift enabled Kim to achieve in ways she had never before considered. Trained in public health nursing and social work, she had no idea of her potential talents and abilities. But she soon discovered another Kim, a woman capable of being a compassionate, articulate, and effective leader.

We've already observed how using the stages of self-empowerment can make miracles happen. First, by accepting a problem, we assume responsibility for it. With networking, we find support to help build self-value and direct our choices. While choosing, we become alert to chances to choose and to make as many of the right decisions as we can. And after a series of healthy choices, we reach a positive shift and enjoy a new way of acting and being.

Unfortunately, shifting can't be rushed. There are no practical tips to help create a shift or to make one happen sooner. The only thing we can do is to work stages two and three conscientiously. By staying close to our supporters and letting them guide our choices, we will make more appropriate choices, preparing the way for a shift to occur spontaneously.

After Kim experienced a shift she wanted to use her remaining time at the hotel to make a difference to homeless women. Even though she was still one of them, she became their empowering example and their spokesperson.

Kim took up her cause first by working for the rights of the hotel women. When she arrived at the hotel she and the other tenants were not permitted to vote because they had no address. She went to court and won their right to vote.

Next she worked with the mothers on supervising their children. "At first I was real hard on the mothers who used drugs, even though life at the hotel was a lot of drugs. But I would never accept drugs as an excuse for not taking care of kids. I felt angry. I prayed to slow my anger because I was trying to understand them, just as I was trying to understand myself."

Then she went to work to get the mothers to look out for themselves. After one mother whose door had been plugged spent the night outside the hotel, Kim went to see her. The mother assured Kim that it had been all right. But Kim said,

• • •

"Do you like people coming in here and walking all over you like that? Don't you have rights?"

Kim thought the women should work as a group to solve problems. "I thought together we could fight this landlord, because he wasn't doing right." When Kim began to hold meetings she was warned by the other women to keep quiet or she'd be killed. Nonetheless, she knocked on doors, spoke to the residents, and set up more meetings. Some days only a few mothers attended and Kim worried that they were afraid to help themselves.

She was also worried that she was spending too much time on causes related to the homeless. "I was willing to do God's work, but I had to take care of my kids, too. You don't just give kids baths and put clothes on them and feed them. You have to build up their minds. They have to be taught. I had given them knowledge of God, but they needed more. Being a mother takes time. And it takes time working with these mothers."

At the point when she was most discouraged by the women's apathy and concerned about her own children's needs, she met Wendy. A social worker, Wendy had heard about Kim's efforts, approached her, and offered to help. Kim said she was too tired and frustrated to fight anymore.

Wendy urged Kim not to abandon the other mothers. "They can't do it without you," she said. "And I'm here now. We'll work together." "Okay," Kim said. "Let's go do it." She decided she would work with Wendy in the mornings and be with her children in the afternoons and evenings.

Kim and Wendy contacted the Legal Aid Society. They brought in advisors on illegal lockouts, illegal evictions, and

♦ ♦ ♦

the hotel's no-visitor policy. They raised money to form the Hotel Tenant Rights Project, set up an office on Thirty-first Street, and held meetings there.

"The mothers began to come to meetings. They were realizing that they had to help themselves, that they had to want it for themselves. They found out our association had some strength. They realized that I just wasn't talking loud and saying nothing. They saw that all-for-one and one-for-all worked. By fighting together against management, they became powerless and we became powerful."

Looking out for others came easily to Kim. "I had always been taught that you're your brother's keeper. If a person needs help, you give it to him regardless."

She set an example for homeless women and also for her own children. She encouraged her children to take care of each other, to get their high school diplomas, and she hoped, some college. She wanted them to have jobs and pay their own rent. She urged them to be independent.

"I told them not to have a lot of babies. I felt blessed to have so many children, but times have changed. I told them it wasn't good for a woman to have a lot of kids. You have to be home or you have to have a family to back you up. If not, you have to go to the system and that's not good.

"I think black fathers have to get involved with their children. I encourage my kids' fathers to spend time, to walk and talk with them, to hug them. More than financial support, that's what kids need, and that's priceless.

"And I try to teach my sons to be strong—I don't want them to be dependent or weak, like their fathers. I tell them, 'You can make something of yourself. You can do it. You can

♦ ♦ ♦

become a doctor. You can become the president of the United States.' I don't want my children to get caught in the cycle of homelessness."

Kim became a force fighting for the rights of homeless women and trying to correct a system that didn't work. She wanted to avert the devastating effects of homelessness on children.

"Many people don't understand that the mothers are here for many reasons: laid off, fire, death, rent increases, or sickness. Some women just don't have enough money for rent. With no affordable housing, lives are being destroyed, especially the children's. How do we know what these children could become—secretary of state or a movie star—if we don't give them a chance?

"The system is supposed to prevent certain things, like homelessness, but it doesn't. And I think it's supposed to get people back on their feet, but it doesn't. It doesn't allow a woman on welfare to make progress. For instance, if she looks and dresses well, they think she's got a live-in boyfriend or she's working a job and not reporting it.

"I'm working on these things and I'm willing to fight for those who can't fight for themselves. I'm even willing to fight for those who won't fight for themselves."

Kim's private war on homelessness began to receive public attention. She spoke on WABC radio and appeared on "Nightline" with Ted Koppel. Mayor Koch of New York City, presidential hopeful Jesse Jackson, and Senator Moynahan visited her at the welfare hotel.

♦ ♦ ♦

"We've had plenty of stars here. They came to me because of my work with the Tenant Rights Project.

"At the Tenant Rights Project, we think mothers should know their rights, learn ways to get off welfare, how to find housing. And that's what we're doing. Giving them that information and being there every day. I'm in my office every morning at nine."

Kim's group publishes a newsletter that outlines their progress on relevant issues. The newsletter also lists workshops the women can take, praises children who've made the honor roll, and notes the women who've recently received high school equivalency diplomas. One mother just graduated from a two-year college.

"We put the newsletters in the women's mailboxes. If anyone has any questions, she can just knock on my door."

Just as Ms. Butler had empowered Kim, Kim was empowering others. She was encouraging them by her example and by working with them, one on one, to take charge of themselves and their children. And just as Ms. Butler had been the catalyst for Kim's high self-value, Kim reassured and coached her children to believe in themselves.

Kim didn't know that by giving so much of herself and mentoring others, she was keeping her commitment to get off welfare and making herself more self-reliant. While sharing what she'd learned, her confidence and self-respect increased. By helping others, she was helping herself handle her own challenges.

"When I can get people to accept themselves," Bernie Siegel writes in *Love, Medicine and Miracles,* "as whole individuals,

♦ ♦ ♦

lovable as they are, they become able to give from an inner strength. They find that unconditional love does not subtract from some limited emotional storehouse. Instead it multiplies itself . . . and sooner or later it returns."

Mentoring has great rewards. There's the satisfaction of observing changes in someone we care for. There's the joy we feel from giving. There's the renewed excitement we get to keep on pursuing our goals.

But when we come to stage five how do we find someone to help? Attendance at any kind of self-help or support group will reveal several people just beginning to work on a problem and looking for encouragement. We can also volunteer in places where there are people who may need help with the issue we are resolving. Or we can call a local hospital or community center for ideas. Or we can ask friends or clergy if they know of anyone who'd like our support.

When we find someone who might benefit from our experience, what should we do? The most effective approach is to share in a direct, personal way what happened to us and what we did to change. There will be more in Chapter Six about how to begin this valuable new relationship.

The importance of the mentoring stage cannot be overemphasized. Becoming an empowering example and working with others can mean the difference between success and failure.

The next newsletter reported that Kim had found two adjoining railroad flats in Brooklyn, with enough rooms for all her children, and a job as a school nurse. Two weeks later she and her children moved to Brooklyn.

♦ ♦ ♦

Today she works as a school nurse at an elementary school two days a week, manages the building she lives in nights and weekends, and takes the train into the city to work with homeless women three days a week.

"By talking to the mothers about myself, I am encouraging them. We try to give one another support. I let the ones still on drugs know that God loves them and that they can make it. I don't want anyone, especially a homeless mother, to feel it's ever too late to change."

PATTY

♦ ♦ ♦

"Hearing what happened to me might help other teens get off drugs."

5

"When I was eight years old my mother had an affair with my aunt Mildred and stopped caring about us kids," Patty said. She sat beside me on a park bench. "I was ten when an uncle turned me on to pot. I started drinking at eleven."

A petite teenager, Patty wore her hair in long brown curls. A hint of pink lipstick and a porcelain complexion gave her an angelic appearance, despite a short denim skirt and tight T-shirt.

◆ ◆ ◆

I had asked the director of a halfway house, a woman who had been instrumental in helping hundreds of addicted women get well, to introduce me to teenagers who'd been successful in dealing with their drug problems. Marie, whose own story is told in Chapter Eight, had high praise for Patty.

As Patty and I talked, facing the pond in the Boston Public Garden, the sky darkened for a summer shower. Mallard ducks swam to the island for shelter. Swan boats, lazily gliding around the island and carrying rows of chattering children, paddled toward the dock. "I used to be an angry, vicious child," Patty said, and shivered. She sat close to the edge of the green bench, her hands clasped around the graying macramé bag in her lap. "I was always running, with no place to go. When I was fifteen I was raped—that was so horrible. At seventeen I got pregnant."

She paused between sentences to glance at me, checking for my reaction. I told her that I understood and that I thought she had achieved an unusually mature perspective on herself. She smiled. As she continued talking, the sun reappeared.

During the next few weeks as I listened to her story, I thought she had come through enough life experiences to fill twice her nineteen years. From grade school on Patty had been looking for a family and someone who would care. She had gone from an abusive mother to abusive men. She had run from person to person, house to house, and drug to drug until she came to the point where she had nowhere left to go but into a rehabilitation facility.

Since then she has become a gentle young woman who is making progress recovering from her dual addiction to drugs and alcohol as well as healing from a traumatic childhood. Patty's optimism and vision for her future springs from these achievements.

Until she was eight Patty lived with her family on the first floor of a three family house, next-door to a funeral home, in a neighborhood on the outskirts of Boston. Her aunt Ellen lived on the second floor. Her half-brother, Jack, her father's son from a previous marriage, lived in the house behind them. Her half-sister, Ann, lived next to Jack.

Patty's early memories were happy: her mother tying up her hair in a ponytail with ribbons and dressing her in Mary-Jane shoes and ruffled dresses; her father, a stocky Irishman who worked as a welder during the day and as a janitor in a bank at night, being gentle with her even when she did something wrong; her grandmother's red house next to an ice cream stand that always smelled of cooked turkey; and her grandmother's round, clear-plastic hassock with the pink roses inside.

In the third grade everything began to change. After school Patty would often find her aunt Mildred, who was married to her mother's brother, at their house. She and Patty's mother sent Patty and her younger sister and brother to the backyard and locked the door. The children banged on the door, wanting to know why they couldn't go inside.

On Saturday her mother and Aunt Mildred always went bowling and took Patty with them. Afterward, they all went to the aunt's cellar apartment. They gave Patty a box of Triscuits and locked her into a tiny, windowless room.

At the end of the school year Patty's mother left Patty's

◆ ◆ ◆

father a note, took their three children, and moved into Mildred's dank basement apartment.

At night Patty's mother hid her car from her husband by parking it on different streets. Patty's father searched every night sometimes until dawn before he found it. He left messages tucked under the windshield, but her mother never responded and the children were not allowed to talk to or see their father.

"That was the worst time of my life. If my mother and aunt didn't like something, they beat us with a strap. We had to go into that tiny room for the night at 6 o'clock. The room had only one cot, so we took turns sleeping on the floor."

The children were treated cruelly. If they talked without permission at any meal, they had food or a drink thrown at them. If one didn't finish eating a hot dog, she was made to eat the whole package. If one didn't like sauerkraut, she had to eat an entire can.

Their mother and aunt wouldn't let the children use the bathroom in the mornings until they were finished. One day Patty's sister couldn't wait any longer and wet her pants. Aunt Mildred got so angry, she wiped the little girl's face with the wet underwear.

"I hated how my mother had changed. I hated the way we were being treated. I tried to be adult and not to show my anger. But after two months I couldn't take it anymore."

Early on a rainy morning in August Patty decided to escape. At four A.M. she tiptoed into the bathroom and brushed her teeth. Oh, God, she thought, I love my mother so much and I don't want to leave my brother and sister. She packed her bag. In the kitchen she printed on a piece of paper "At Gram-

• • •

ma's, bye, Patty" and tucked it under a stack of towels, hoping no one would find it.

"I ran out of the house, scared to death, like I was being chased by someone with an ax. I ran five miles in the rain and hid behind a car or a bush each time a police car drove by."

Soaking wet, Patty arrived on her grandmother's porch. She sat down on the front steps, shivering, and wondered what to do. Finally she got up to ring the bell and her grandmother's smiling face appeared in a front window, behind the white lace curtains. "I came to move in, Gramma." Her grandmother hugged her.

That morning Patty held court on her grandparents' big bed watching TV. Her grandmother brought up a tray of breakfast and her grandfather helped her into dry clothes. Before her uncles left for work, they came in to see her. She soon fell asleep.

Two hours later Patty woke up and, through the window, saw her mother getting out of a police car. When she heard her mother coming up the stairs, she burrowed under the covers. "Do you want to come home or don't you?" her mother shouted. "I don't." Patty said. She listened to her mother walk down the steps and watched the police car drive away.

After spending the summer with her grandparents, Patty moved to her father's for fourth grade. He took her to see her sister and brother, who were still living with her mother, but during those visits Patty refused to speak to her mother.

Patty found new relationships with her father and his sister,

◆ ◆ ◆

her aunt Ellen. "After school, before I did my homework, my father and I played Battleship. I always let him win, because he let me do anything I wanted and get away with it. And I got to know my aunt Ellen that year. She tried to give me values and teach me sayings like—"It's better to give than receive because God always returns it to you." I knew she loved me because she always tried to look out for me."

Before Patty's fifth grade year, her father worried that Boston's school integration laws, requiring the busing of minority groups into white neighborhoods, would heighten racial tensions. Fearful of rioting, he sent Patty to live with her grandparents, who had moved to a suburb west of Boston.

Patty had trouble adjusting socially and academically to the new school. Not sure where she fit in, she became preoccupied with her appearance. "Most of the girls were rich. One group had those monogrammed clutch bags with the wooden handles and colors you could change. I wanted one, too. And I wanted a pair of designer jeans, but my grandparents said Wranglers were good enough for me. So I wore regular jeans and three long, dangly earrings in each ear. That year I got into big-time stealing."

On her last shoplifting spree at a mall Patty stole one of the clutch bags she coveted and six records. She slipped rings and earrings into her socks, necklaces into an eyeglass case. Nervous when she thought an overweight woman with red rouge had seen her stealing, Patty dropped a bottle of Charlie perfume into her purse and headed for an exit. The woman followed, talking into her walkie-talkie. Patty rushed out the door into the arms of a waiting policeman. She was handcuffed and taken back inside to the security office. She refused to

• • •

give her phone number, but the police found her grandparents and brought them into the store. When it was finally over Patty was so shaken she resolved never to shoplift again.

"I was ten that year. My uncle, who lived at my Gramma's, said not to worry about how I looked, that I could be grown up in other ways. He showed me how to smoke pot with his big waterpipe. He told me I wouldn't get high, but I did and I liked it.

"The next year I started taking sips out of my grandfather's liquor bottles. If my grandparents weren't home, I helped myself. When my grandfather left to pick up my grandmother from work, that gave me twenty minutes. It was time enough for me to get down a few slugs from his bottles. When they were home I drank my grandmother's cologne. And because it was my chore to clean the bathroom, I could get high upstairs almost any time with my uncle's bong."

When she visited her father and couldn't get a drink, she drank his after-shave lotion. Sometimes she made coffee brandy at her father's, which he thought was Nestle's Quick.

Soon after Patty started using drugs and drinking, her personality changed. She already had a low level of confidence, felt insecure, and didn't think anyone truly cared about her, although her grandparents tried hard to reassure her. With a tendency toward addiction, Patty's use of drugs made her turn against everyone, especially herself.

By the time she was fourteen and in her last year of junior high, Patty was failing most of her classes. She skipped school often and, when she did go to school, she skipped classes. She spent most of her time in the smoking area, where students went to get high, or in the girls' room, where the girls shared whatever pills they had.

◆ ◆ ◆

To buy drugs she needed more money than the five-dollar weekly allowance her father gave her. When she saw her sister and brother she bullied them for their allowances. She took money from her grandfather's change box and saved up her lunch money. "I would rather get high than eat. Being on drugs was like that.

"Because of drugs I lost the little confidence I had. I began to think I was ugly. I became angry, depressed, and cried all the time. I started carrying a knife and doing crazy things. I became vulgar and vicious. I chased people down the halls, knocked them against walls, and tried to crush their faces in. I made a lot of enemies. I just didn't care."

The summer before she started high school Patty was drinking so much she blacked out for the first time. "It happened at a party. There was like a light switch going on and off. I'd be in one room, then another, but I couldn't remember anything in between. I was fifteen and told myself to act cool. I didn't want anybody to know I was a rookie."

When she woke up the next day she could recall only isolated moments from the night before and was scared. In her pocket she found a crumpled paper with a phone number, but she couldn't remember whose number it was. She dialed the number and thought the man seemed surprised to hear from her, but he was friendly. They started seeing each other on the weekends Patty stayed with her father. If she couldn't sneak out to meet him, he climbed in her bedroom window.

"He was twenty-three and the first guy I ever had sex with. I didn't know what I was doing and thought sex was boring. He never took me out. To him I was just a piece of ass. But to me, he was somebody. I'd always been crazy about boys. I wanted a boyfriend but never thought I'd have one. I didn't think I was pretty enough."

That fall Patty met often with her guidance counselor, but she continued to use drugs and to get poor grades. A few months later she was suspended. She was transferred to a technical high school in another suburb with only thirty students, all of whom had been suspended from other schools.

"I was, like, home. Everyone took drugs. We did speed, methadone, dust, and coke. I loved it. Those kids were the only people I knew who drank as much as I did, but I always drank faster."

That spring Patty's class took a field trip. Going to the Museum of Fine Arts in Boston, she used acid in the van. By the time she entered the Impressionist Gallery of Monets, Cézannes, and Cassatts, Patty felt like she could walk into or taste each painting.

Later that day on the way to Plum Island, while the students listened to Led Zeppelin, the trees along Route 128 seemed to be moving to the rhythm of the music. "When I got to the beach I was like in heaven. The sky looked navy blue. The waves were like rolling in to me."

When Patty began stumbling up a sand dune, one of her teachers, who was a recovering alcoholic, noticed. Pam asked if she could help. They had talked several times before, and even though Patty had always refused Pam's offers, she kept Pam's phone number in her purse. Patty told Pam that she was fine and carefully climbed up the dune.

Although Patty thought she was doing what she wanted, she was miserable. Drugs and drinking were alienating her

♦ ♦ ♦

from her family and friends. She knew she was losing Aunt Ellen, whom she adored, but she couldn't stop herself.

She considered suicide. She took her grandfather's pistol out of its case and stood in front of her bedroom mirror pointing it at herself. "Who'd come to your funeral?" she asked into the mirror. Shaking her head, she put away the gun.

There didn't seem to be any way to stop herself from drinking and using drugs, until late one January afternoon during sophomore year. She had gone with a new group to the river's edge in Dedham. After drinking her share of a quart of vodka and smoking pot, she passed out. When she woke up the sun had set, the other girls had gone home, and she was alone in the dark with the boys. One of them asked her if she had a pipe. "Sure, I always do. Why?" "Let's get high," he said. He held the sleeve of her jacket and pulled her down the bank into a shed. Inside there was a piece of stained carpeting and a candle. He lit the candle and they sat down.

Abruptly, the young man ripped off her jacket and knocked her backward. Patty pushed him away, kicked, and yelled at him to stop. But then she passed out. When she opened her eyes, he was on top of her. When she opened her eyes again, he was pulling up his pants.

The next morning Patty lay inside the shed, covered with snow, feeling sick, cold, and frightened. She turned her head and saw on the ground next to her her purse and mohair jacket covered with vomit. Horrified, she got up and ran. When she got to a Dunkin' Donuts, she took Pam's number and a dime out of her purse and slid into a phone booth.

◆ ◆ ◆

Shaking, Patty sat on a stool waiting for Pam. She covered her face with her hands and tried to pick the sand out of her eyes. Every few minutes she slipped off the stool to look out the window for Pam.

When Pam arrived, Patty told her she didn't want to go home and face her grandparents. All she wanted was a ride to school. Pam shook her head and ordered breakfast. Patty felt too sick to eat anything, but used the coffee to warm her fingers. After hearing what had happened to Patty, Pam suggested that they go to an A.A. meeting. Patty refused.

Pam drove her to a nearby discussion meeting, anyway. Patty looked around at the banners on the walls—One Day at a Time, Live and Let Live—and then sat down at a long, rectangular table next to Pam. As talk on the day's topic of remorse and guilt began, Patty leaned toward Pam and whispered loudly, "That's me. I feel like a piece of shit."

For the next few weeks Patty went to A.A. meetings and to church. She still denied that drugs were a problem, but she didn't drink. It was difficult for her not to drink when most of her friends did. "I prayed every day—to be strong, to have a better life, to live for God instead of myself. I prayed for miracles, like some angel would come to me and tell me what my life should be like. My grandparents, who knew about my drinking, were so happy with me. Everyone in my family said I'd done a three-hundred-sixty degree turn."

♦ ♦ ♦

Unable to deny the inevitable any longer, but with all the resistance of a normal teenager, Patty began to recognize that drinking, at least, had become a problem for her. Although she had been upset by her own behavior and the loss of her friends' and family's affections, she couldn't get to acceptance. It wasn't until the morning she woke up in a snow-covered shed that she realized drinking and drugs had made her so vulnerable, she'd been raped. Accepting was just the beginning for Patty, a chance for her to remodel her misshapen life. Acceptance was necessary if she wanted to change.

She didn't know that her other grandfather, a half-brother, and two uncles were alcoholics and that she, too, carried a genetic predisposition toward addiction. And she didn't know what alcoholism was or that her behavior matched quite well the National Council on Alcohol and Drug Dependence's most recent definition. "Alcoholism is a primary, chronic disease with genetic, psychosocial, and environmental factors influencing its development and manifestations. The disease is often progressive and fatal. It is characterized by continuous or periodic: impaired control over drinking, preoccupation with the drug alcohol, use of alcohol despite adverse consequences, and distortions in thinking, most notably denial."

Most of us, at one time or another, suffer the consequences of denial, no matter how elaborate, convincing, or articulate our presentation or protestation. Denial can reduce our anxious reactions and insulate us from painful situations.

How can we learn to break through such an appealing, powerful defense and accept our circumstances just as they are?

♦ ♦ ♦

When we deny we disavow, repudiate, or make light of the truth and the seriousness of an event or our behavior. And there's an attractive aspect to denial that might keep us hooked. It's hard to give up something if it makes us a victim and gives us pay-offs, such as extra attention, sympathy, or a license to indulge in self-pity. But not surprisingly, there is a downside—the cost and the consequences of denial.

When it appears obvious that the cost is greater than the pay-off, we may wonder why people continue to deny the truth. Yet when the problem is our own, it's not so easy to be objective, logical, and rational. It may seem easier to conjure up reasons to continue destructive behavior.

And we persist in denial to avoid what is too painful to bear, to feel, or to experience. "Denial is the shock absorber for the soul," Melodie Beattie writes in *Codependent No More.* "It wards off the blows of life until we can gather our other coping resources."

When we're ready to face what is happening, or has happened, we may move into a period of anger. Still not yet ready to accept, we express our frustrations and feelings about our problem. After anger we may try bargaining, or making promises, as a means of restitution or for getting what we want. When that fails we may fall into depression. Relief and peace eventually follow. And we know acceptance, at last. We know that what is—is. Whether or not we like it, we accept that this is it, this is our life, these are our circumstances.

"Acceptance is never simple," Janet Woititz says in *The Struggle for Intimacy,* "but it gives you the freedom to change and enhance your life."

When Patty accepted that drinking was a problem she made

◆ ◆ ◆

progress and felt more freedom. But by clinging to drugs she delayed her recovery and was led back to drinking, more than once.

After Patty had been sober ten months an old friend invited her to a party. "We haven't seen you for a long time," she said. "All you do these days is crack open the Bible. Why not crack open a few beers?"

Patty was in the mood for a party. She promised herself she wouldn't drink, and she didn't. But she did get high. Stoned, Patty invited everyone to her father's empty apartment for another party, where she drank and passed out. When she woke up she was on the sofa with a young man she didn't know.

Horrified by what she had done, Patty wanted to start over. She called Pam and they went to meetings together for the next few months.

"I thought the people at meetings were incredible. I felt good; I felt like I belonged. I stayed away from the kids at school who drank. And I couldn't wait to see my friends in A.A.—they were the only real friends I had."

Although she had made mistakes, Patty was reaping the benefits of networking. Pam, who understood what Patty was going through and what she needed, was her first empowering example.

Because Pam had successfully confronted her own problem with alcohol, she understood how Patty felt fighting denial.

◆ ◆ ◆

Pam knew how hard it was for Patty to accept that she had a disease and could no longer drink or use drugs. And from her own experience Pam knew that Patty would need help making daily decisions and would need someone to affirm her.

With Pam's help Patty began to like herself more, and her self-value improved. "Identification is one of the central processes by which we build a self," Judith Viorst tells us in *Necessary Losses.* "The people with whom we identify are, positively or negatively, always important to us. And although we may clearly recall a conscious decision to emulate some teacher or movie star, most identifications take place outside of our awareness, take place unconsciously."

Especially in the beginning, if we feel uncertain about our chances for success or are unsure of ourselves, we'll find enormous comfort knowing that someone else has accomplished what we want to do. And more importantly our motivation will increase because someone else cares that we make it.

In the early stages of changing, having someone closely aware of our activities makes it harder to stand still or backslide. Besides ourselves, there is someone else we don't want to disappoint or let down.

Until we get to the place where we can see our chances to choose and are readily making positive choices, there's nothing wrong with behaving as we think our empowering example would, or would like us to. In time, as we become accustomed to a new way of acting, we won't feel so dependent on support. But there will never be a time when we won't need some support, even when we are supporting someone else—especially then.

◆ ◆ ◆

Still using drugs, Patty lashed out at those closest to her—her grandparents for setting a curfew and her father for not caring enough. With nowhere to live, she moved into a roach-filled apartment with a seedy group who used drugs.

Patty stopped seeing Pam and her A.A. friends. Without support, she began drinking again. She didn't care about anything but drinking and drugs and dropped out of school.

During the Christmas holidays she went to her father's house and spent time with his three children from a previous marriage. She was attracted to Jack, her twenty-year-old half-brother. "I told him I was an alcoholic but not that I was a drug addict. We got high all the time, and I slept over at his apartment, in the house behind my father's."

Patty became friends with Jack's sister, Ann, who was Patty's half-sister. When Ann invited Patty to live with her and her husband, Al, Patty hoped that they could become her new family. She didn't know that Al, who weighed three hundred pounds, was a drug addict with a terrible temper, severe depressions, and problems with the police.

When Ann went out to Bingo games, Al secretly supplied Patty with coke and mescaline and terrorized her by making passes at her. If she was high, she didn't care. One night Ann returned from Bingo and found Patty and Al stoned, sitting at the kitchen table playing cards. "You guys are on drugs!" Ann hissed. Ann was frightened by the scene and warned Patty not to tell their father that Al was giving her drugs.

Not surprisingly, Patty became afraid of both of them. She could hear them criticizing her late at night and wanted to leave. But because she had alienated everyone else, her grandparents and her father, she had nowhere left to go.

A friend suggested that she get drunk so she could go to a detox and from there she would try to get her into a halfway house. Neither Patty nor the friend knew that such a scheme wasn't necessary to be accepted into treatment. So the friend bought Patty a six-pack and a pint and Patty drank.

A few hours later, when Patty was drunk, the friend left her at the door of a city detox. The only other people there were street people. Patty had to dress as they did in men's pajamas, a striped paper bathrobe, and paper slippers. She was angry and wanted to leave.

"But there I was—the little girl with ponytails who was sixteen, going to be seventeen in a few weeks. Everyone said I was cute, but I had a dirty mouth. I called the nurses douche bags and told them to give me my fucking medication. That first night they gave me so much Librium, the doctor had to wake me up the next day."

Five days later she was on her way to Shepherd House, a halfway house for women.

"When I got in Shepherd House I didn't plan to get sober. I just thought of it as a roof over my head. I was sure no one there liked me, so I acted like I didn't like them. I wanted to call Al and say, 'Hey, get me outa' here.' But I didn't. I just did whatever chore I had to do as fast as I could, went to workshops, and never said a word."

After a few weeks Patty felt good and looked better. She didn't feel as angry. She liked how she was changing and started to care about herself and other people.

◆ ◆ ◆

Patty called her grandparents to tell them where she was. Her grandmother was happy to hear from her and relieved that she was getting treatment. But her grandfather laughed and said, "You won't stay long. You'll always be a gypsy." Patty suddenly felt upset. She didn't like the idea of herself as a gypsy.

When she hung up she spoke to the director, Marie. Marie made a special arrangement for her to stay at Shepherd House a full year, so that when Patty left she would be eighteen, old enough to move into her own apartment.

With her new plan in mind, Patty worked hard on her recovery. She got up early, dressed, and went downstairs for exercise and meditation. She did her chores carefully and thoroughly. In workshops she participated and tried hard to describe what she was feeling. She attended group counseling sessions, met with her individual counselor, and went to A.A. meetings in and out of the house.

For the first time Patty was choosing actions that were good for her. Until then what had appeared to be action or conscious choosing was actually reenacting. Whether running, rejecting, attaching, or attacking, she had been recreating situations reminiscent of the traumas of her early years.

Patty had been not only reenacting but also acting in a way that drew attention to herself. "Children raised in dysfunctional homes," Claudia Black said in *Repeat After Me,* "typically play one or more roles within the family structure. These roles are identified as: The Responsible Child, The Placater, The Adjuster, and The Acting Out Child." Black described The Acting

◆ ◆ ◆

Out Child as angry, confused, and scared, one who acted out his confusion in ways that would get him attention, even if it were negative, at home, school, or on the streets.

While Patty played The Acting Out Child she was able to get some of her needs met. Family and friends worried about her. Sometimes she was the center of concern. But her antics didn't provide her with feelings that she was secure, lovable, or loved.

We might consider how we are handling unmet needs and what we are doing to compensate for them. Are we turning to self-destructive substitutes? Rationalizing our choices? Missing chances to choose?

When Patty entered the halfway house she took a chance to choose, even though her heart wasn't in her choice. She went through the motions of new behavior and, in time, desire and commitment followed. But before she could make a positive shift she relapsed after several poor choices—not unusual for someone at this stage.

Marie encouraged Patty to study for a GED, a high school equivalency diploma, instead of getting a job right away. "That was great. When I graduated some of the women from the house came. One of them even lent me a dress to wear. I felt so proud of myself."

Patty met with a counselor from the Massachusetts Department of Rehabilitation, who promised to help her find financial aid for college, but not until she had been sober a full year. In preparation for college, she took a typing course at a junior college.

♦ ♦ ♦

Patty was receptive to her counselors' support and she also became friends with two women residents at the house. Because she admired Marie she became close to her as well.

"They all encouraged me. At first, when I wouldn't let anyone near me, they let me know they cared anyway. They were good to me. That was beautiful. After a while I could talk to them and be myself. I loved them all.

"My old personality was slowly melting away. I really wanted to make it. I wanted things to work out. I was like—finally my life is going good and getting better."

Patty asked one of the older women she had met at an A.A. meeting outside the house to be her sponsor in the A.A. program. Daily her sponsor supported Patty's efforts to recover. Patty followed all of the advice her sponsor offered, except the suggestion not to become romantically involved or to make any big decisions until she had been drug-free and sober for a year, giving her time to clear up mentally and emotionally.

Defiantly, seventeen-year-old Patty went out with Jake, a twenty-two-year-old man. They spent nearly every weekend together and she thought she had finally found stability and someone to care for her. "He was the most important thing to me. We had a lot in common. He was an alcoholic who was trying not to drink and drug, too. During the week he sent me cards and love letters."

When Patty discovered that she was pregnant she was terrified and hoped Jake would marry her. "But Jake wanted no part of it. I kept hoping he'd let me have the baby, but he insisted I have an abortion. So I did."

Patty didn't want Marie to know what had happened and told her only that she had decided to leave the house and move

• • •

into an apartment with Jake. They both had full-time jobs, and they shared both expenses and housework.

A few months later Jake started drinking again. His personality changed. He stopped helping Patty with the housework and refused to carry his bags of laundry to the laundromat. He stayed out late most nights.

When he announced that he was leaving her, Patty begged him to stay. She had put up with his faults because she needed to be close to someone. There was no one else she could talk to the way she talked to Jake.

But that night she returned after work and found all of his clothes and furniture gone. He had taken everything. For the next few days she did nothing but cry, seeing only images of Jake.

It had been nine months since she'd had a drink or used drugs. She didn't want to endanger her chance to go to college or lose the progress she had made. She had a choice. She could reach out to the women who had helped her before or she could try to handle her overwhelming feelings of abandonment, loneliness, anger, and being unlovable alone.

Patty didn't ask anyone for help. Two days later she was drinking.

"I hated myself. I went out with a lot of guys. I drank with them and after they left I'd cry all night, thinking about Jake.

"During the day I worked as a cook and because of drinking my mind started getting mushy. I couldn't think. I'd go over

♦ ♦ ♦

to get the carrots and come back with a cabbage in my hand. I had the shakes and started to think of an afternoon drink.

"But I didn't really want to be drinking. So I tried to get hold of myself. I made myself remember what I was supposed to be doing. I talked out loud to myself."

Patty wanted to stop drinking but knew she couldn't do it alone. She called old friends from A.A. and asked them to help. They gladly took her to meetings and called several times a day.

Just as she was beginning to feel better Jake appeared at her door. He was drunk. When he kissed her the taste of alcohol made her want a drink, too. He had come for sex and she gave it to him. The next morning she hated herself for giving in and thought a drink might erase her awful feelings.

"This time I knew I had a choice. I called my sponsor and she said to pray. I looked out my apartment window and said, 'God, help me. Help me to forgive Jake.' I got down on my knees and said out loud, 'God, please help me not to drink today.' "

Every day for the next few weeks, Patty prayed. And she also called people in her family and asked for their support. Despite previous problems with her, each one responded to Patty's attempts to get well and make amends. Her father called every day. Her favorite aunt, Ellen, came to see her. Even her mother, who had seen Patty only a few times in recent years, encouraged her. Her grandmother and the uncle she had smoked pot with, who was still smoking pot, went to see her. With this support and encouragement, she got through Thanksgiving, Christmas, and New Year's Eve without one drink. Because she was sober, their caring enabled her to care about herself.

In January Patty got a job as a hostess in a restaurant. "I couldn't believe I was doing it. That job gave me such confidence. I started looking nice and feeling great. Guys were asking me out and, if I didn't want to go, I could say no. It felt beautiful. I did what I wanted. I joined a health club to work out. I was making friends. I felt dynamite. It was like this is what it's all about."

After months of hard work, resisting temptation, and making good choices, Patty's attitude shifted noticeably. "There's nothing as wonderful as starting to heal. Waking up in the morning and knowing that nobody can hurt you if you don't let them," Bass and Davis write in *The Courage to Heal,* about an abused woman's recovery. Patty, too, felt confident and optimistic.

Shifting came not only from picking herself up when she slipped and fell but also from her willingness to forgive both herself and others. Through forgiveness Patty let go of what was keeping her vulnerable to further destructive choices. For as long as she blamed someone else for her trials, she would remain a victim. As a victim, she gave away her power to help herself and to change.

As soon as Patty stopped blaming her parents and Jake, she discovered that she could put herself in charge of her own life. From there she was free to make the choices, including forgiving herself, that led her to make a positive shift. Finally feeling happy, confident, and directed, she was not about to

♦ ♦ ♦

let anyone or anything disrupt her recovery. No matter what happened next, her shift would shield her.

That summer Jake got married and Patty was understandably depressed. She daydreamed about the good times with him, forgetting the painful times of feeling abandoned and alone. When the thought came that drinking and drugs could quell her memories, she carefully reviewed what that would cost. She could lose the respect of her family and support people, and she would lose her dream of going to college. Patty easily decided not to drink or use drugs.

After Labor Day she celebrated a full year of sobriety. Her A.A. group gave her a cake with one glowing candle and her family threw a party. Through Mass Rehab, Patty was awarded a four-year scholarship to the University of Massachusetts in Boston. Patty was overjoyed. She began working as a part-time bookkeeper to help pay her other expenses and that September she began college as a full-time student.

"I hadn't been to school for a long time and the whole first semester I was like a sponge. My average right now is three point seventy-five. I feel terrific and know I can make something of myself."

She is studying in a program to become a counselor to teens who have drug problems. Once a week Patty goes back to her high school to talk informally to individual students. She and Pam run a self-help group for teens that meets at the school. Patty speaks at A.A. meetings and attends workshops on addiction. She has become a sponsor to a sixteen-year-old, and she is working with the uncle who started her on pot and

• • •

her younger sister, who is beginning to show signs of a drug problem.

Without the mentoring she received, Patty would not have become capable of giving to others in a similar way. The help she received came from individuals and groups. And most of the people who guided her were also recovering from addictions.

In *Psychological Trauma*, Dr. van der Kolk referred to the way others can influence an individual's survival. "People survived either because others helped them or because they themselves had to think of others." Both of these aspects, as they relate to one another, make survival and recovery possible.

Patty didn't have to try hard to think of others. Her desire to work with teenagers flowed naturally from her own accomplishments. While most of her friends were still wrapped up in themselves, Patty's painful past propelled her to reach out and take an interest in others.

As much as she liked the satisfaction that came with helping someone else, she had learned that she couldn't give away what she didn't have. And she wouldn't have anything to give if she didn't make her own recovery a top priority.

Through all stages of self-empowerment, but especially at this mentoring stage, being attuned to our own needs is critical. This is the time to be sure we aren't becoming complacent. We can ensure that by staying in close contact with our empowering examples, by watching our choices, and by being alert to our chances to choose. This is the time for taking care of our own physical, emotional, and spiritual requirements, as well as those of others.

♦ ♦ ♦

Patty works daily on her own recovery, which is always necessary but even more challenging for someone with a history of abuse. Out of her own painful experiences she has become a role model for other teenagers. She has become capable of empowering them to make turning-point changes in their lives. In so doing, she ensures her continued growth.

"I know what it's like to be a teenager on drugs. I know how hard it is to get off, what the temptations are, and what it's like not to feel good about yourself. I want to help kids get their lives straightened around. Mine is wonderful. Hearing what happened to me might help other teens get off drugs. I believe I can make a difference. So far for me, things are good, and I'm looking forward to the future."

STEPHANIE

♦ ♦ ♦

"After helping other women get their lives back together I now consider my divorce a gift."

6 "When I met Ben he was blond, charming, a presence," forty-year-old Stephanie told me. "In many ways he reminded me of my father. I'd always wanted to marry someone like my father, but someone who needed me and wouldn't leave me for someone else."

I'd heard part of Stephanie's story from a writer friend who had done a feature piece on her, "Suburbia with Style on a Shoestring." While reading a draft I was struck by what lay

◆ ◆ ◆

just below the surface. Underneath the accolades for a woman who had ingeniously recreated a semblance of her former lifestyle after a divorce from a rich man was the poignant story of one woman's survival.

The more I learned about Stephanie the more I realized her experience was one that many women, married or divorced, could identify with. Like many of her generation, she had put her family ahead of herself and her professional interests. Even though her own needs weren't being met, she had been willing to sacrifice anything to keep her family together and her marriage intact.

Before Stephanie arrived for the first of several days of interviews, we'd had so many preliminary conversations on the phone we felt like friends. She had sounded so self-assured and strong that I was surprised by her fragile appearance. She was thin, with long black hair, light blue eyes, and a white complexion. To illustrate her story, she brought photo albums, her Bible, and a copy of "Great Is My Faithfulness," her favorite hymn.

She had suffered through years of living with a womanizing husband and then through a demoralizing and devastating divorce. During divorce negotiations and an unexpected court battle over the children, in which she lost custody of one of her daughters, she became anorexic.

Today Stephanie has recovered from her eating disorder and her other painful losses. Despite self-doubts and fear, she has learned how to combine single parenting with a career and even a social life. She has been asked to remarry more than once, but doesn't feel ready yet.

In the process of rebuilding her life she became a role model in areas where few existed. She now works with other divorced women, showing them how to juggle their responsibilities and balance their lives.

"I've been through all of this for a purpose," she said. "I know it was to make me a better person. I've seen many lives change, especially my own."

"From the time I was four I knew that my parents were unhappy. Children sense when things aren't going right."

She described her father as cosmopolitan, a bon vivant who looked like Clark Gable. He was an investment counselor who held a seat on the New York stock exchange. But he worked long hours and was away so much, Stephanie felt she never really knew him.

She thought her mother was brilliant and beautiful. She loved to have people in and always set an extra place at the table on holidays. She was an artist as well as a talented second-grade teacher.

"My mother put up with my father's terrible temper and she knew there were other women. She thought if she just kept working hard on the marriage their problems would go away."

When Stephanie was eight years old, her father abruptly left and never returned. He married a twenty-five-year-old woman, gave up his seat on the stock exchange, and moved to Florida. Her mother was distraught. She managed to teach during the days, but after dinner she would go into her room and close the door.

Stephanie felt alone and abandoned. She missed both her

♦ ♦ ♦

father and her mother. She missed taking art, music, and riding lessons. And when her mother had to move to a small house outside of the city, she and her brother missed their friends.

"I was allowed to see my father only once a year for dinner. The first time I worked myself up into such a state, I threw up in his fabulous car. Four years later he died. And I wasn't allowed to go to his funeral.

"While other kids were under their covers with flashlights reading books, I was under the covers talking to God. I hoped he was there."

Stephanie went to a small college in Missouri. She worked hard preparing to be a teacher and student teaching in a ghetto area, had fun at sports events being a cheerleader, and made many new friends.

She was as interested in her friends and classmates as she was in herself. She thought that a young man who lived in town, one of eleven children, was smart. She found him a tutor and helped him apply to colleges. She thought another young man who hung out with a gang had potential. She studied with him, urged him to apply to law school, and was pleased when he was accepted. As much as she enjoyed feeling needed and helping other people, she wanted someone to care about her.

During sophomore year she met Ben. He'd also grown up in New York City on the Upper East Side. "Ben didn't have many friends. He'd been raised by servants and I thought he needed someone to really care for him. When I listened to his problems—he'd been expelled from several prep schools—I felt I could help. And he seemed to like me. He brought me huge bouquets of flowers and dozens of presents. Many times

• • •

I found him waiting for me in front of my dorm. In junior year he asked me to marry him."

In the spring of senior year Ben had a nearly fatal accident when he was hit by a truck while riding his motorcycle. He stayed in the hospital several months for a series of operations, including a hip replacement and plastic surgery. When the doctors released him his mother said she was too busy that summer to care for him, and Stephanie's mother invited him to recuperate at their house.

"All summer we talked about getting married and he gave me an engagement ring. We planned to have our wedding in the fall. Even though in some ways he seemed strange since the accident, I was happy and completely committed to him."

Near the end of the summer, when he was well, Ben disappeared for two months. He had told Stephanie he wanted to go mountain climbing alone in the west. She waited to hear from him, but he didn't call or write.

In October, after she'd given up, he suddenly appeared at her door. He told her he couldn't live without her and still wanted to get married. "My mother thought we should wait, but she understood my attraction to him. He was a mysterious man, much like my father. I loved him so much and thought he needed me."

In December they married and moved to Missouri to live near the college they'd attended. While Ben finished his senior year Stephanie studied for her masters degree in education. She wanted to be a teacher like her mother.

But Ben wanted to start a family right away, even though he spent little time at home. The day Stephanie brought their

♦ ♦ ♦

first baby, Juliana, home from the hospital, Ben went out for the evening. When Stephanie and their second daughter, Jessica, arrived home from the hospital, Ben left again and didn't return until eight the next morning. When he came in, freshly showered and shaved, she was so tired after being up all night, she felt like crying. Instead she said nothing. But to herself she said, "If I just try harder, if I just love him enough, he'll be with us more."

Ben not only continued to spend most of his time away, he also became abusive. After they moved to New York, where Ben worked as a stage manager, they were invited to spend the summer with his parents at the Jersey shore. The only weekend Ben appeared, he was brutal. He threw furniture around their bedroom and hit Stephanie. When the cook heard the noise she called the police. The police were concerned about Stephanie's bruises and swollen face and asked if she wanted to press charges. She shook her head. She said that her husband was just overtired and overworked.

Other outbursts made her consider leaving him. But she was terrified of being alone and doubted that she could support herself with two young daughters. And Ben controlled their finances so tightly that Stephanie hadn't learned to pay bills or balance a checkbook. She had become so dependent, she didn't think leaving was an option.

Six years later, however, Ben announced that he was leaving her and did. When she didn't hear from him for several weeks, she reluctantly called a lawyer.

The lawyer urged her to look for any evidence of other women. In the back of a desk drawer, under manuals on stage rigging, she found a notebook in which he'd written a description of all his conquests. He'd moved in with a college

♦ ♦ ♦

girl while she was in the hospital having Juliana. When Jessica was born he was seeing an actress. Even the summer before they were married he'd gone mountain climbing with a girlfriend. Some of the women had gotten pregnant and had had abortions. He had told them all grandiose stories about himself.

"I was so angry and hurt I was nearly out of control. My worst suspicions had been confirmed. I was completely devastated.

"I didn't think I should talk to anyone about it. I wanted my mother to be happy thinking I had a perfect marriage. I couldn't bear having my friends know that my husband had left or that he'd had affairs. The worst feeling was thinking I didn't have any choices."

Several months later, Ben appeared at her door on Mother's Day. He told Stephanie that he knew he was emotionally disturbed but didn't know what to do. They both thought his problems had started after his motorcycle accident. He begged her to take him back.

She went to her room and came back with his notebook. "I realize this is past," she said, "but I can't go on without talking about it." "Those women didn't mean anything," Ben said. "They all thought I was a much different person than I was. I hated myself and had to do that because it made me feel important."

Stephanie agreed to let him move back in and to help him, if he promised to get counseling.

While sailing in a regatta in Newport, Rhode Island, Stephanie and Ben couldn't find a hotel room and asked their friend David, a minister, if they could stay with him. As soon as Ben left to check their boat, David asked

♦ ♦ ♦

Stephanie how things were going. His question surprised her. She didn't think anyone knew they had problems. For the first time she talked. And she wept. When David suggested that they pray, she didn't know if she could. She had never prayed out loud before. But then she closed her eyes. "Lord, you know my life is falling apart and things are a mess. I've been going around in circles and need help. I want my marriage saved and things to work out for us. I've got to know if you are there."

In the fall Stephanie joined a church. "I made a decision to ask God to come into my life. I studied the Bible and found a chapter in Proverbs describing a wife. 'She will do him good and not evil all the days of her life. . . . Strength and honour are her clothing. . . . She openeth her mouth with wisdom: and in her tongue is the law of kindness. She looketh well to the ways of her household, and eateth not the bread of idleness. . . .' I wanted to be that woman."

Despite Stephanie's efforts Ben stayed away from home, even during the Blizzard of '78. Without heat or electricity because of the storm, Stephanie tried to conceal the pain of wondering where he was while making dozens of Valentine cards with her daughters and cooking in the fireplace.

When he returned he announced that he had been with his mistress, a twenty-four-year-old chorus girl who had once been a prostitute. She was pregnant and refused to have an abortion.

Distraught, Stephanie prayed for patience. Although Ben promised to give up his mistress, he spent most of his time at the theater or in his study with the door closed.

After church one Sunday, Stephanie and the girls returned home and Juliana went into the apartment first. "Mommy,

• • •

we've been robbed," she yelled. The rugs, paintings, furniture, beds, pots and pans, vacuum cleaner, and silverware were gone. All that remained were two canvas chairs and clothes, strewn on the floor.

Stephanie found Ben's note on top of the clothes: "I have to do what I have to do."

Stephanie had a hard time accepting that her marriage was over. Committed to her husband, and believing that he needed her, she had always considered it the woman's responsibility to make a marriage work.

Earlier, when the truth would have been too painful to bear, she had fallen into minimizing and rationalizing Ben's behavior. She hadn't been ready to accept the loss of her ideals for marriage. And letting go of her dream would have meant another loss that she was not even aware of. Because her husband was elusive, unpredictable, and undependable like her father, Stephanie had hoped, unconsciously, that Ben's love would compensate for what she had missed with her father.

During the times she had endured abusive circumstances, Stephanie's self-value eroded. Without a positive self-value, her fear of abandonment magnified. Afraid of being left, as her mother had been, Stephanie tried everything she could—perseverence, forgiveness, devotion—to hang on to her marriage and her husband.

"What (that) is about," John Bradshaw wrote in *Lears,* "is trying to do everything for somebody else, to the point of giving up one's own reality and in some cases one's own life, to manipulate someone into loving you so you won't be abandoned. It has nothing to do with growth and caring and nurturing somebody so that he can grow spiritually. It just enables the loved one to be weak and the lover to be abused. It is a very real addiction to a certain kind of destructive relationship."

While trying to hang on to Ben and save her faltering marriage, Stephanie had become a codependent. Although usually associated with members of an alcoholic's family, codependents appear just as often in other dysfunctional relationships. "It is a dependency on people," Melody Beattie wrote in *Codependent No More,* "on their moods, behaviors, sickness or well-being, and their love. It is a paradoxical dependency. Codependents appear to be depended upon, but they are dependent. They look strong, but feel helpless."

Even though the term codependency is relatively new, the dynamic it describes may be a familiar one. Involvement in a relationship in which one is working hard to please someone else while suppressing her own needs has become all too common. The other person's problem takes priority and one attempts to take over and manage its resolution. If there are signs of codependency in our own lives, we might question whether our efforts are intended to change or rescue the other person or if we are trying to hold on to the relationship.

Stephanie's fear of being abandoned kept her from facing difficult issues. By overlooking what was happening, she inadvertently perpetuated the problems. She not only enabled their marriage to continue in a dysfunctional way, she also let an obsession with her husband's needs keep her from taking care of her own. She thought her only course was the one he directed. She gave up her power to him and when she couldn't act he did it for her.

♦ ♦ ♦

But after accepting that the marriage was over, Stephanie was able to begin the process of empowering herself. She began to understand that she, too, was responsible for the breakdown of her marriage. She realized that her own fears of being left behind had made her blind to the issues in front of her. She learned that as long as she felt victimized, she had no power to change. Although it would take time before she felt confidence in her ability to be a single parent, she began by accepting the truth of her situation. Next, she turned to networking and using support.

Stephanie called her mother, who arrived with furniture and kitchen equipment. She called David and then confided in three close women friends. All of them urged her to divorce right away.

"I knew they were right, but I was so afraid I couldn't make it on my own. One moment I'd think I was better off without him. The next I went back to thinking that Ben would change his mind."

When Ben's mistress had a baby boy he decided to marry her. "At that point I became totally incapable. I couldn't think straight. I couldn't function. I had to rely on my friends. I fell apart at the slightest decision and cried for no reason. I was so disoriented, I couldn't make change for a dollar. The first time the lights went out I didn't know it was because I hadn't paid the bill. When the accountant asked if I had my taxes ready, I said, 'Have what ready?' "

Physically weak and distracted by her problems, she had a car accident. The insurance company paid Ben two thousand dollars for the repairs, but he kept the money. Stephanie was

• • •

reduced to riding her bicycle to get groceries and visit her lawyer.

During months of bitter negotiations they went to court several times. At the final session the judge awarded Stephanie custody of the girls, modest child support, and her car. No longer able to afford their seven room apartment, she and her daughters moved to a smaller one nearby.

The day after the divorce was final, Ben remarried. He and his young wife moved to Atlanta, Georgia, built a large house, and began having more children.

Stephanie hated having to send her daughters to Georgia for their occasional visits with Ben. At the end of one visit, when she called to arrange for their return, Ben said, "I'm not returning them. I'm keeping them."

Stephanie filed an injunction to get her daughters back. Ben initiated a custody suit. The court investigated Stephanie's family and Ben's family. As she endured the inquiries, probing, and waiting, Stephanie depended on friends. They assured her that she was a wonderful mother and had nothing to worry about.

In court Stephanie listened to the judge conclude that she was indeed a fit mother but because Ben was married and had more luxurious, suitable accommodations, he would grant them joint custody. The judge further suggested that Jessica live with her mother, but because Juliana was fourteen he would allow her to choose where she wanted to live. Juliana looked from her mother to her father, then to the floor. Almost inaudibly, she said she'd live with her father. Ben grinned and said loudly enough for Stephanie to hear, "Well I've got one. Now I just have to get the other." Stephanie felt as if she'd been stabbed.

♦ ♦ ♦

"I was in such pain. I felt betrayed, angry, and resentful. Sometimes I'd go out into the woods near my mother's house and scream. Other times I'd go into the closet where no one could hear me and cry. I'd say, 'God, I just can't stand it! How much more can I take?'

The only thing she felt she had control over was what she ate. She usually weighed 108, but her weight dropped to 80 pounds. "It wasn't that I didn't want to live or that I was trying to punish Ben. I was just afraid of what was ahead."

Despite her weight loss, she didn't consider herself too thin at first or notice how pale and gaunt she looked. Some days the only thing she would eat was a chocolate chip cookie or a tablespoon of maple syrup. After Jessica went to school Stephanie lay in bed with the sheet pulled over her head. But within a few weeks she hated to see herself in the mirror. Her eyes looked yellow, a thin layer of hair covered her body. She didn't realize that she had become anorexic or that she was dangerously ill—or know that therapy could help.

Finally, too weak to get out of bed and too sick to care for Jessica, Stephanie called her mother. She didn't want anyone else to know about her condition. Her brother carried her into the hospital and her mother took Jessica home with her. After a month of counseling and care, Stephanie gained enough weight to return home.

Then Ben threatened to sue for custody of Jessica. Terrified and desperate to feel control over something, Stephanie again stopped eating. Ill, weak, and malnourished, she returned to the hospital.

This time she let those supporting her help. Her friends and

♦ ♦ ♦

David came to see her. David told her several times what a beautiful, talented person she was and how sad he was to see her destroying herself. She listened.

For the first time she felt new resolve. Alone in her hospital room, she cried. With sunlight from her window streaming across her bed, she thought of a Bible passage: "If a woman felt loved, she'd do anything for her husband, but if a woman didn't feel cared for she'd rise up and care for herself."

"At that moment I decided I could and would care for myself. Before then I couldn't understand why God was doing these things to me. But suddenly I realized why. He wasn't doing these things *to* me, he was putting these things in my life because they were what I needed to make me a better person.

"Finally I saw that I wasn't going to survive with the poor-me's. If I was going to survive, I *had* to rebuild my life.

"To start again I would be dependent on God. I would let him run my life. I would still have choices, but I would do his will. I would walk at his heel or by his side. I knew that if I raced ahead of him I'd make mistakes. I prayed to look forward, not back, and to become self-sufficient. I felt myself getting stronger."

Networking and faith had enabled Stephanie to make it this far. David, her mother, her friends, and, at times, her lawyer and her daughters, had pulled Stephanie through the most devastating time of her life. She was learning to depend on a higher power and on healthy people, people who loved her and cared. In time this dependence would reemerge as inner strength and dependence on herself.

The catalyst for some of her early changes, her minister friend David became an empowering example. He had encouraged her to talk freely and he let her know that it was healthier to express her feelings, that it was all right to be supported. Above all, he had helped her to develop her childhood faith into a spiritual force.

While trusting in God and taking suggestions, Stephanie had learned to let go of her self-will. "Self-will means believing that you alone have all the answers. Letting go of self-will means becoming willing to hold still, be open, and wait for guidance for yourself," Robin Norwood explains in *Women Who Love Too Much.* "It means learning to let go of fear (all of the 'what ifs') and despair (all of the 'if onlys') and replacing them with positive thoughts and statements about your life."

Before learning to let go, Stephanie had rationalized, sometimes concealing her will in seemingly reasonable justifications. But once she realized that relying solely on her own devices didn't bring the results she wanted, she turned to others for guidance.

Stephanie learned that answers are available from several sources. By being open to possibilities, solutions we never imagined may unfold in front of us. By observing and listening, we may hear just what we need from talking to a friend or from something we read.

As a result of being receptive to new ways of thinking, Stephanie began to create a life far more satisfying than the one she had been clinging to. As her self-value improved, increased confidence enabled her to recognize more choices. She not only became aware of her choices, she also became eager to make use of them.

◆ ◆ ◆

When she left the hospital Stephanie was ready to take charge of her life. She bought a calculator and learned to pay bills. She balanced her checkbook and kept records for taxes.

Stephanie and Jessica found a smaller house outside the city and worked together repairing and furnishing it. They painted and wallpapered. They re-covered an old chair and sofa. Stephanie hung black and white engravings, "end of the day estate sale bargains," on the walls. Jessica salvaged a dollhouse that a neighbor had put out for trash pick-up. An older woman from their church gave them a rug, two chairs, and four place settings of china. They found the rest of the things they needed at thrift shops and church rummage sales.

Before Christmas they decorated the house for the holidays. They planned menus, prepared soups and casseroles, and invited friends for dinner. They sewed and painted handmade gifts.

Stephanie knew she couldn't manage without working and began to look for a job. An older woman in the neighborhood needed someone to take care of her. Stephanie got her up, bathed her, and fixed her hair. She took her out in a wheelchair to museums and restaurants. Helping someone else took Stephanie's mind off her own problems.

She found other part-time jobs helping a friend cater private parties, working in an antique shop, and doing fund-raising for a nonprofit organization. She took evening business courses.

When she was offered a job with a leather company, she didn't know if she'd fail or succeed. "But I had to try. Even though I was scared to death, I decided to take the risk. It meant flying all over the country, so my mother helped me with Jessica."

A year later, a competing firm hired her and promoted her to marketing specialist for the northeast territory. The next year a textile company called to ask if she'd consider a position working with designers and architects. She competed with sixteen other candidates for that job and won.

Two years later she established her own upscale catering business. Jessica and Juliana when she is visiting, help their mother cook, serve, and decorate.

"I love my work. These jobs brought out abilities I didn't know I had and gave me a lot of satisfaction. My confidence is great and I feel ready to take on even greater challenges."

Motivated by her determination to survive, Stephanie was choosing to become independent. When she began this stage she struggled with each choice, but as she moved closer to a shift she didn't need to deliberate. She knew what to do.

Her ability to make healthy decisions was the result of working through the process. When she was entrapped by a view of herself as victim, she'd had no energy to act; she could only react. She assumed that she had no other course but the one Ben directed and passively played out her part.

Stephanie had begun to change when she let go of the idea that others were responsible for her circumstances. She stopped seeing herself as the victim and Ben as the villain. With her decision to become responsible for herself, she began to experience, for the first time, a feeling of power. She felt

♦ ♦ ♦

high knowing that she actually had chances to choose. And when a choice turned out well, she liked its effect and the person she was becoming. Her self-value soared. Each accomplishment led to yet another more challenging choice with the probability of a favorable outcome, an impossible scenerio for a victim.

As Stephanie discovered, the cost of being a victim is high. Living as a victim means buying into the idea that we have no power, that our fate is determined by someone else, even that we are willing to sacrifice a satisfying life. But with the decision to stop blaming someone else for our woes, we become accountable for our actions or inaction. We can opt for actions that are in our best interest, not someone else's, even if that approach feels uncomfortable at first.

"The sense of pleasing herself," Jean Baker Miller wrote in *Toward a New Psychology of Women,* "has been a very rare experience for most women. When they attain it, it is a newfound joy."

And, indeed, it was a newfound joy for Stephanie, who had once put everyone else's needs ahead of her own, to reconcile her need to care for others and her need to be cared for. By caring for herself she began to emerge as a whole person, with strengths and weaknesses, able to give and to receive love.

"At the same time I was learning how to support us I was also learning how to juggle all my responsibilities. With a daughter and house to take care of and a full-time job, I had to find a new kind of organization. I'd been organized before—teachers always are—but I had to figure out a different way of doing things.

◆ ◆ ◆

"I began by managing my time carefully. I plan a time for nearly everything. I even plan times to talk to my daughter. But on that I'm very flexible. Sometimes when we have dinner alone together nothing important comes up. But if I arrive home with a full briefcase and Jess needs to talk, I put my work aside.

"I also spend as much time as possible with Juliana when she visits. For a while she seemed to have a chip on her shoulder, like her father. Our relationship has been stressful, but I know in time she'll understand what I've been through.

"Handling stressful situations has also been a learning process for me. I try to remove as many stresses from my life as possible. And instead of worrying about what could go wrong, what possible catastrophes are out there, I try to plan for them.

"And I surround myself with people who pull me up. My friends are people I get energy from and can give energy to.

"Another thing that helps me is to sit down at my desk on Sunday nights and review the week. I go over the mistakes I made, the positive things that happened, and evaluate how I handled situations. If I got a letter from Ben that week that upset me, I tell myself that there is nothing I can do about it.

"Now when I talk to him, I don't feel hatred. I think if God can forgive him, I can forgive him. Ben has seen the changes in me. I've learned and grown. I even think I've come through this better than he has. My life is going well."

Stephanie felt serene and sure of herself. After shifting, it almost seemed that her struggle was over. She still had decisions to make and hard tasks ahead, but she could now do them with greater ease and a sense of inner harmony.

♦ ♦ ♦

Stephanie's shift resulted not only from professional and personal accomplishments but also from her willingness to forgive Ben, as well as herself, for their failed marriage. She could have taken the position that anger and hatred toward her former husband were justifiable responses to what he had put her through. She chose instead to forgive him.

"Forgiveness is wonderful," Melodie Beattie writes in *Co-dependent No More.* "It wipes the slate clean. It clears up guilt. It brings peace and harmony. It acknowledges and accepts the humanness we all share."

After forgiving Ben, Stephanie felt free to create a new life. She no longer depended on him; he no longer had the power to hurt her. She had moved so far along in the self-empowerment process that she felt even greater confidence, enough to take risks and to indulge in dreams.

As it was for Stephanie, the time following a shift can be an exhilarating one for us. We feel the rush of victory. After what we have accomplished, we have a feeling of mastery of our own life, at least. We believe in ourselves. We trust ourselves to resist a reversal in thinking and acting. Our focus is on our present and future, even though we may not know exactly what shape our life will take.

Shifting presents all kinds of options and chances to venture into areas we never thought possible before. It is the time for reaping rewards, after months and perhaps even years of hard work. We'll have not only the courage but also the desire to compose our own life.

"Composing a life means integrating one's own commitments with the differences created by change. . . ." Mary Catherine Bateson writes in *Composing a Life.* "Because we have an altered sense of the possible, every choice has new meaning. . . . The real challenge comes from the realization of multiple alternatives and the invention of new models."

Stephanie had supporters but she didn't have any role models, other single working mothers to show her the way. She had to experiment with her own formulas and design her own style. But while she figured out for herself how to combine raising her daughter with the demands of a career, a house, and a social life, she became a role model for other women who were wrestling with similar challenges.

As Stephanie reflects on the course of her life, she talks about her hopes for the future. "I dream of marrying a wonderful man. We will pray together and go to church together. It's important to me that he not base his whole identity on his career or achievements. Because he'll know God, he'll see himself as a good person, regardless of his job."

She is philosophical about the relationship between pain and growth. "The Bible says that God gives us the desires of our heart. And sometimes we aren't aware of our deepest desires. I want to always be open to God's guidance. There are times when he wants us to go through trial, through trauma, and that's where we're supposed to be at that time. We may try to pull ourselves out of a depression when God wants us to be sunk—in that depression—for a while, because from there a new insight will come."

She attributes her growth and change to her spiritual foundation. "When I look back, I can see God's hand in all this. Even the times when it didn't feel like he was there, he was. He was guiding me. When God begins his work, he finishes it. He has made my success."

♦ ♦ ♦

As the result of the newspaper story on Stephanie, her activities at church and in the community, and her successful career, other single working mothers heard about her. She welcomes their calls about jobs, new responsibilities, and relationships. Most of the women ask specific questions and Stephanie offers practical suggestions.

To meet these needs further, Stephanie has set up an informal support group that meets once a week at her house. The group gives its members an opportunity to talk about what they need personally and to tell what they have already learned. They offer encouragement and receive support from one another. The group also provides a center of resources for child care, legal services, and professional networking.

While mentoring Stephanie is taking her skills as a caregiver, once her only source of identification, beyond her family unit. "Women not only define themselves in a context of human relationship," Carol Gilligan wrote in *In a Different Voice,* "but also judge themselves in terms of their ability to care. Women's place in man's life cycle has been that of nurturer, caretaker, and helpmate, the weaver of those networks of relationships on which she in turn relies."

By reaching out to serve others in her community, Stephanie continues to experience something of that cycle. Because she is regarded as a role model for the divorced women and mothers she is guiding, she must remain strong. Although it appears that the women who seek her out are dependent on her, she in turn relies on them to maintain her growth.

When we are ready for mentoring, we can begin by making ourselves available in situations where our experience might be of use to someone else. We won't rush in waving a flag about reforming the world or having all the answers for a particular problem. But we can introduce ourselves and have a conversation, keeping the focus on ourselves. We can tell what happened to us, what we did to change, how we view ourselves and our future now. If our listener shows interest and begins to talk about herself, we can offer a phone number for a further conversation. It's important to let the other person ask for assistance. And if she does, we can begin to build a supportive relationship, one that will also strengthen us.

Stephanie felt strengthened by her work with the women in her support group. "After helping other women get their lives back together," she said, "I now consider my divorce a gift."

J O N I

◆ ◆ ◆

"When I couldn't walk, I never dreamed of becoming a world class athlete. Now I'm coaching other women."

7 Joni had fallen in a skiing accident when she was twenty-nine, fractured her neck, spine, and skull, and nearly died.

Thirteen years later, she raced across the finish line at the Ironman Triathlon in Hawaii in 1985, setting a world class record for masters women. She had completed a course that included 2.4 miles of swimming, 112 miles of bicycling, and 26.2 miles of running in just over twelve hours.

When Joni described her moment of victory she said, "I was filled with more self-confidence and self-respect than I

♦ ♦ ♦

have ever felt in my life. For the first time in my life, I felt I had accomplished something."

Although Joni's win was a personal triumph, it received national attention. "A Winning Attitude," the story in the *Boston Globe,* praised her accomplishment. The lead sentence: "Joni has done the impossible." The caption under the photograph of a woman with long, blonde hair: "From a body cast to a championship."

Before our first meeting I had expected that she would be quite physically fit. But when she arrived at my office in shorts, T-shirt, and ponytail, looking like a teenager, it was hard to imagine that she had a teenaged son. It was nine o'clock on a summer morning and she had just driven three hours. We talked until eight-thirty that night, with only one break—for me to make lunch and Joni to run. Then, with seemingly limitless energy, she jumped into her VW and drove three hours back home.

During our marathon conversation, I learned how she had empowered herself to win two different times. First, after her tragic accident, she followed the stages to return to a nearly normal life. Then again, she turned her withered and deformed body into that of an admired athlete. In this chapter we'll observe Joni using self-empowerment the first time, then go with her step-by-step as she becomes a triathlete.

"I am the least likely person to achieve what I did," she said. Although I wouldn't agree with this modest assessment, it is Joni's sentiment. I am repeating it because it is one that many of us might identify with.

♦ ♦ ♦

As a child, living on a farm in rural Indiana, Joni was expected to do the difficult, whether she wanted to or not. She walked three miles to school and three miles back home, even through blizzards. During the week her Dutch Reformist parents taught her to study hard and to do her chores, then on Sundays to sit quietly alone. She was rarely allowed out to play with friends; she could never go to movies or dances.

"My mother was the strong person in our family. We were all afraid of her. She thought life was supposed to be tough. She believed we were put on earth to suffer and she made us suffer.

"My dad saw life entirely differently. He would take me in his truck and we'd do something fun together, like go to a carnival. He made me feel special and showed me I could have good times without feeling guilty. If it hadn't been for him, I probably would have stayed there, gotten married, and turned out just like my mother."

After high school, when her friends were getting married and having babies, Joni wanted to go to college. At Hope College, a Dutch Reformed school in Holland, Michigan, her world expanded. She met young women from other parts of the country. Her roommate, from Washington D.C., had been an aide to Robert Kennedy and encouraged Joni to reach out further. "I learned from her that there was a lot more to life than what I knew. I just had to find it. I thought the only way I could was through a career."

After college she did graduate work to become a registered medical technologist. Despite recriminations from her mother,

• • •

Joni lived alone in an apartment and had a car. "I was really on my own, made my own decisions, and felt some confidence. I didn't have to account to anyone. I was very serious about my studies and worked hard at the hospital, learning how to draw and analyze blood, doing bacterial cultures and blood counts. I graduated at the top of my class and got a job paying eleven thousand a year, which in 1964 was a fortune."

She started dating Ken, a young man who'd also graduated from Hope College. He had grown up in Connecticut and wanted to return to the East Coast to start a career in advertising. Joni wanted to move east, too. "We would bounce our dreams off each other. When we decided to get married, my mother was so relieved she gave me a big wedding."

After their wedding they loaded a U-Haul and drove east. Joni found a job in a hospital and Ken started work in New York City. They moved into a town house in Greenwich, Connecticut, bought a Porsche, and two years later, their son Bryan was born.

"I loved the baby so much and, for the first time, felt I understood what love was. Ken and I were good friends, but there wasn't any kind of romantic love in our relationship. Something was missing for both of us. We both knew it wouldn't last."

When Ken approached her with his plan to make a career change, producing rock concerts all over the country, Joni encouraged him to go after this new dream without her. They agreed to remain friends but to separate. A year later, with no argument over a settlement, they had an amicable divorce.

♦ ♦ ♦

A single mother with a three-year-old son, Joni too started a new career—as a model in New York. She began seeing Michael, a stockbroker, whose family owned a ski house in Stratton, Vermont.

Michael invited Joni, a good intermediate skier, to Stratton for a winter weekend of skiing. On Saturday, after stopping for lunch, they headed back to a lift for their first afternoon run. Halfway down the mountain, Michael slowed his pace and called back to Joni, "If we turn here, we can go to a chair lift that will take us to the top again. We don't have to go all the way down."

Joni followed Michael as he glided ahead of her down a gentle hill. When he reached a flat section of trail, she noticed that he lost his balance slightly as he turned right toward the chair lift. Just before she got to the same place, she saw that skiers turning right had built up a lip of ice on the left edge of the trail.

"I hit the lip and it acted like a ski jump. I flew up and out into the air, suspended over a ravine. I looked down and wanted to grab hold of something, but there was nothing—it was all air and all white. I must have looked like a fool to this guy who was so important to me. I saw a tree with very few branches growing out of the side of the ravine coming at me. I knew the tree would stop me, but I didn't want to hit it with my face. When I jerked around, I heard my back crunch, grind, and break. Then everything stopped.

"The next thing I knew I was in this big place that had no boundaries. It was quiet with soft light and I was walking toward the light. There was a giant movie screen with pictures

♦ ♦ ♦

of me in a cradle, me when I was two and three, my grandmother, and my parents. I saw all the people who'd ever been in my life, everything I'd ever done, the good things and the bad, and then it was gone. I was walking in a long hallway toward this incredibly bright light. It was so peaceful.

"Suddenly I thought, I've got to go back for Bryan. I wanted to stay in the soft warmth, but I forced myself to turn away from the light and go back."

Joni opened her eyes. She was lying in the snow and felt a burning sensation along her back. Michael stood over her, shouting frantically for help. He thought she was dead.

The ski patrol carefully put her onto a sled and took her to the first-aid station at the base of the mountain. The doctor on duty quickly called for an ambulance to transport her to the nearest hospital.

In the ambulance she felt herself slipping away. The attendant monitoring her status said, "Don't go to sleep, Joni."

"It hurts . . ." she said, and closed her eyes.

"Talk to me. Tell me your name. Tell me anything, anything. Hang on," he repeated. She used all of her strength just to breathe.

At the hospital she could hear the medical staff discussing her case. She heard the doctor say, "Call her parents. She won't make it through the night."

"When I heard that I wanted to speak, but I couldn't. I can't die, I thought. I just can't die. I can't leave Bryan. I lay there. I worked hard to breathe. I concentrated on staying awake. I knew if I went to sleep, I might not wake up. I just had to stay with it. I had to fight it. I began to get really strong. I could feel myself getting strong inside."

♦ ♦ ♦

Sandbags were placed along both sides of her body. Joni's neck and head were extended with traction apparatus.

A doctor leaned over her and spoke gently but clearly. "You can't move at all now. You must lie still. Would you like to know what we saw on the X rays?" Joni let him know with her eyes that she would. "Your neck is fractured in three places," he said. "You have a collapsed lung, multiple fractures in your back, and a fracture on your skull, but the worst is that your dorsal spine area is completely crushed."

From the fearful look on her face, the doctor knew she wanted to know if her spinal cord had been damaged. "We don't know yet," he said. "There's too much bleeding and swelling around it to tell." When he left the room she lay motionless, wondering if she'd ever walk again.

That night Joni looked up and saw a window above her. She told herself that she would live through the night so she could see the morning. That would mean another day. For the next five days she consciously renewed her decision to live one more day, just long enough to see the light.

The next few days she tried to recall people and past events, but there were gaps in her memory. With her fingers she tried writing the alphabet on the sheet, but forming the letters was difficult. She couldn't remember some letters and had forgotten numbers, as well.

She was being given morphine for the pain and begged them to stop. The staff agreed to let her try. "I wanted to see if I could deal with the pain myself. So I taught myself to handle the pain by pretending to leave the pain on the bed and raising my body above it."

◆ ◆ ◆

Joni could have escaped awareness of her condition and her misery by letting drugs lull her into oblivion. Instead, she chose to confront a devastating reality and intense pain.

She was glad to be alert when her close friend Susan, who had been caring for Bryan, brought him to see her. Susan held Bryan, still in his snowsuit, up over his mother's head so she could see him.

Blinking away tears, Joni looked up at her son. It was an important moment. From that time on she was sure, no matter what came up, that she would do whatever she could to recover and live a normal life.

When she was stable enough she was moved to a hospital closer to home. For another two months she lay flat on her back, wondering when she'd be able to take care of Bryan, whether she'd ever work again, how the accident would affect her relationship with Michael, who visited every weekend, and how she would live when she left the hospital.

Until that spring, she lay flat in bed. Then one day a doctor and two nurses put her into a metal and plastic cagelike brace that went around her head and neck, over her shoulders, and stopped at the top of her thighs. She couldn't bend, so they raised the head of the bed and eased her into a kind of sitting position. They guided her legs over the side of the bed and helped her to stand.

While the doctor and nurses held her upright, the doctor said, "I want you to take one step. Just move your right foot forward."

Joni looked down at her feet and tried to move her right foot, but nothing happened. "What's wrong?" she asked him.

"You've got to think about it," the doctor said. "You've got to really concentrate on what you're doing." He spoke

◆ ◆ ◆

close to her, as if to get the message to her brain. But Joni couldn't take a step.

Several days later she tried again and that time she managed to shove her foot a few inches. "Look, I did it!" she said, very excited. She attempted another step. "Stop. Whoa. That's it," the doctor said. "One step, now back in bed. It's going to be hard for a while, but it will get easier."

Each day she endured the struggle to get into the brace that protected her spinal cord and, with the help of a doctor and a nurse, she practiced taking steps. The effort to make her legs move was hard, hard work. But she didn't consider giving up. She tried again and again.

In two months, she could walk with the support of the brace and was able to leave the hospital. Since she still couldn't take care of Bryan by herself, Michael's family invited her to live with them. Several months later, Joni and Michael moved to an apartment.

"For the summer I wore the brace under a loose shirt and pants. The brace held up my spine. Without it, the shattered bones inside could have cut into my spinal cord. I was five feet seven before the accident, but after I was five three and severely hunchbacked. It took a while but I finally found a surgeon willing to talk to me about correcting my deformity."

During the consultation Joni listened to her options. Without surgery she would wear the brace the rest of her life and could eventually become paralyzed. If she chose surgery, it could take up to nine hours. He would open up her back and possibly her chest. He would open up her hip and scrape bone off her pelvis to place over her spinal cord. He'd remove the bony fragments left inside. If the operation went well, she would still have a slight hunchback but be able to walk without the brace. If there were problems, she could wake up paralyzed or not at all.

Joni went home to think about it. She talked to Michael, her parents, and to her best women friends and decided to take a chance on the extremely risky surgery.

On the morning of the operation the doctor stopped into her room to prepare her for her first conscious moments after surgery. "When you wake up," he said, "don't be frightened if you have bandages down the front. It means we had to go in from both sides. And don't be afraid if you can't move your legs, that may only be temporary."

Ten hours later she was wheeled back to her room. Still fighting an anesthetic fog, she looked up and saw a nurse standing over her. She was smiling.

"I knew from her smile that I was okay. She grabbed my hand and said, 'Honey, you're going to be fine.' "

The doctor arrived and told her that in two weeks he would take out the stitches and put her into a cast from her shoulders to her thighs. She would have to wear the twenty-two pound plaster cast for eleven months.

By January, a year after the accident, Joni had learned to get around fairly well in her cast. "I could do everything but bend. If I dropped something I had to pick it up with my toes. I couldn't take a bath, but I could stand in the tub. I was able to get into my car by first putting my right leg straight across the seat, then lowering myself down and going in as one chunk. I had to kind of lean back to get my other leg in."

♦ ♦ ♦

She was still living with Michael and worried about their relationship. She knew the past year had been hard on him, in many ways. She feared their relationship was changing, because she couldn't relate to him in a sexual way. She appreciated his loyalty and friendship. And when she was ready to care for Bryan, she was grateful when he rented a larger apartment so Bryan could live with them.

"I took care of Bryan, ran errands, shopped for groceries, and took care of the house. By spring I went back to work full-time on the night shift."

Doctors at the hospital were impressed with Joni's determination and asked her to visit patients suffering from disabilities. Joni happily complied and always liked how she felt when she left patients' rooms. Though not yet cognizant of why this was so, she noticed a renewed surge of energy.

In September she drove to New York to have the cast taken off and took Bryan with her. Bryan watched while the doctor cut the cast in two long pieces and got ready to lift his mother out. The doctor helped her to a standing position. Bryan hugged her and said, "You look like Mom again."

Joni walked over to a full-length mirror. "My skin was a mess and my muscles were atrophied. I looked over my shoulder and saw the scars on my back from my neck to my lower back. I looked at myself sideways. The hump was smaller. My breasts were completely flattened out. The inches I'd lost were above my waist and I looked like a short-waisted person."

Numb and vulnerable, she left the doctor's office. On the hour and a half drive back to Connecticut, she felt the pain in her back she would feel the rest of her life.

At home she took a luxurious, long bubble bath, dressed in

clothes she hadn't worn in two years, and looked forward to seeing Michael. As she prepared dinner, he walked into the kitchen.

"You look great," he said. "But I don't know what to do. I don't know if I can touch you."

"Don't worry," Joni said, trying to conceal her disappointment. She knew he had been looking for an apartment, and it was only a matter of time before he would move out. "I'm so glad you were willing to stay with us, at least until the cast came off. You've been wonderful."

For the next few days Joni and Michael talked about their relationship. She understood his indecision and his need to be independent. She thought the accident had made her less attractive and worried that she would be a burden to any man because of constant pain.

"If someone wants to go, I've never been one to hold on. It hurts, but you live and time makes it better. If you try and make somebody do what you want and not really what they want, it only makes the situation worse.

"After Michael moved out, I resolved to rebuild everything. Bryan and I would just have to do the best we could."

Vaughn, a resident at the hospital, heard that Joni was no longer living with Michael and invited her out. An all-American swimmer in high school, he offered to teach her to swim. He took Joni and Bryan swimming often and by the end of that summer Joni could swim four laps in a small pool.

Several months later Vaughn asked Joni to marry him. She hesitated because she thought she was still too vulnerable. Even with her reservations, Joni married the young doctor.

◆ ◆ ◆

"Vaughn was wonderful with Bryan and wanted to adopt him. Bryan's father Ken and I had stayed close, and he agreed to the adoption. All of us were good friends.

"Vaughn worked hard as a surgeon in New York six days a week. I wanted to be with him more, but he said he needed to work that hard for us. I asked once to go away for a weekend, but he explained he would lose too much money not operating, so we didn't go.

"We bought larger and larger houses and ended up in one with twenty-six rooms and nine bathrooms. I felt like a guest because we had a live-in housekeeper and cook. My husband didn't want me to work, so I poked around in stores but didn't like shopping or spending money. I was just there.

"I felt I was losing myself. Vaughn had a strong personality. He was the center of conversations at parties. He picked out what he wanted me to wear and I just went and looked nice. I was nothing more than a doll."

Articulating and accepting her dissatisfaction posed a dilemma. Joni had worked hard to achieve a solid sense of who she was. From an easily intimidated child, she had turned herself into a courageous, strong woman capable of risking all she had become for all she could be. Accustomed to achieving, she disliked an aimless existence. As her self-value diminished, she looked carefully at her circumstances—the woman she had become, how she lived, and what she thought of herself. Although she appreciated her husband's support and didn't want to lose him, she thought she had to challenge herself beyond what she was doing.

Joni not only acknowledged that a nonproductive life-style

didn't work for her, she also knew that she would have to make the changes. To change her circumstances, she first had to accept them, exactly as they were.

"Acceptance does not mean adaptation," Melodie Beattie writes in *Codependent No More.* "It means, for the present moment, we acknowledge and accept our circumstances, including ourselves and the people in our lives, as we and they are. It is only from that state that we have the peace and the ability to evaluate these circumstances, make appropriate changes, and solve our problems."

Without accepting our circumstances just as they are, no one can change. We learned, along with Joni after her accident and from the other women in this book, that a problem can't be solved until there is acceptance of its existence and of the responsibility for working on it.

Joni didn't blame anyone for her situation. If she wanted to be happier, she knew it would be up to her to make that happen. "Most of us have the ability to be far happier and more fulfilled as individuals than we realize," Robin Norwood writes in *Women Who Love Too Much.* "Often, we don't claim that happiness because we believe someone else's behavior is preventing us from doing so."

As Joni thought about what she might do to fill her vacant days, she also considered her husband. She didn't want to alienate or upset him.

Running had become a popular sport and Joni bought a pair of running shoes. She talked about running with her husband. He didn't think it was a good idea but agreed to let her try.

◆ ◆ ◆

"My first time out I ran down the driveway and it hurt so much I couldn't breathe. After half a block the pain was agonizing.

"I had to somehow deal with the pain. Right after the accident I'd learned to separate myself from the body that was hurting, to get myself away from the pain. So I taught myself to take a step out, to run in front of myself, and to leave the hurting person behind.

"Embarrassed and hoping no one would see me, I went to a local track. I ran three times a week and by spring I could run up and down hills for three miles.

"That summer people in the neighborhood and at the country club noticed that I looked good and asked what I'd been doing. All I needed was someone to pat me on the back and I was ready to go out and do it again.

"I kept running and on my daily run I really felt content. I felt like I could do anything out there. I ran hard and had a great feeling afterward that lasted until the next day."

When she could run five miles, she entered her first race. And won! It had been such a struggle, the achievement thrilled her.

When she could run longer distances, Joni entered marathons. She ran the New York City Marathon in 1979 and 1980, the Bermuda 10K and Marathon in 1981 and in 1983, and the Philadelphia Marathon in 1983.

Her success with running led her to try another sport. For additional endurance and fitness, she started riding her bicycle, until she could ride twenty miles a day.

"I spent a lot of time at my local sporting goods shop. The owners had been supportive all along and when I became fairly good in a third sport, they suggested I try a triathlon.

♦ ♦ ♦

I took an application home with me, but didn't send it in."

Joni wasn't sure she was up to triathlon competition. She had been watching a younger man, Mark, one of the first triathletes in the country, train on the streets of Greenwich. She was fascinated and wondered if she should try. But when she saw a televised triathlon showing a middle-aged mother of two running, cycling, and swimming long distances, Joni felt even more encouraged. She envisioned herself doing the same things.

"If she could do it, I could do it."

Joni's motivation was the result of networking and feeling support from many people—local athletes, the sport shop owners, even her hesitant husband. She had also been influenced by observing others and had been empowered by their examples.

Support, plus her competitive achievements, had helped Joni restore her self-value. She liked the woman she was becoming and believed in herself once again. Her self-value improved further as people praised her and encouraged her efforts. The more she succeeded the greater her self-value became and the greater her self-value became the more able she was to respond to the energy of others.

Maintaining her strong self-value would be essential to going on, but there were times when she felt uneasy. She worried about competing publicly, afraid she'd let herself and others down.

"For women, however, it seems that the sense of worth of the self has not been allowed to develop, or has been allowed to develop only inadequately," Sanford and Donovan write in *Women and Self-Esteem.* "Though many women, spurred by the revival of the feminist movement, are presenting themselves more proudly and confidently in public, in the privacy of their own minds too few seem to have favorable images of themselves and hold themselves in high regard, (or) consider themselves truly valuable."

For Joni, keeping her self-value high would depend on her own determination as well as other people's feedback. Even during contentious times ahead and moments of doubt about whether to continue competing, she did what she could to keep her self-value high.

"The self-concept or self-image is the set of beliefs and images we all have and hold to be true of ourselves," Sanford and Donovan wrote. "By contrast, our level of self-esteem (or self-respect, self-love or self-worth) is the measure of how much we like and approve of our self-concept. Or, as we've heard it put, 'self-esteem is the reputation you have with yourself.' "

At this point we might look at the reputation we have with ourselves. How do we feel, for example, about our performance at work, the way we relate to others, or the way we take care of our appearance and surroundings? Is there anything we would change? Our responses will provide clues to our level of self-value.

Improving self-value can come not only from networking but also from the choices we make.

Excited and nervous, Joni made a decision to enter a triathlon. "I wanted to start with a small one, far from home, where no one would know me. My husband worried

◆ ◆ ◆

that I might get hurt, so he arranged for a friend, Guy, to enter with me. Guy was to swim, bike, and run beside me, not as a coach, but to keep me from getting hurt."

By seven A.M., at the triathlon in Tampa Bay, Florida, Joni had checked in. After numbers had been written in black magic marker on her arms, thighs, and calves, she set up her equipment for each event in transition areas and headed to the beach for the start of the swim. Each age group had a different colored cap—Guy, in his thirties, wore red and Joni, in her forties, wore yellow.

"I was so scared I was shaking all over. My hands were ice cold. I thought I was going to throw up. Suddenly we heard "Go!" and everyone ran into the water.

"As soon as I got into the water, someone swam over my legs, an arm came down on my head, and another arm knocked off my goggles. I was terrified. I treaded water while I tried to put my goggles back on. I tried to swim but I couldn't get my arms to come out of the water. When Guy found me I was crying. I wanted to go back, but he told me to relax. So I tried again, slowly.

"After a while it got easier. I passed the yellow caps and reached the red caps. Everything was fine until I got to the cement breakwater where the water was going back and forth. I started going back and forth and the smell and taste of gasoline in the water made me sick. But I forced myself to finish.

"I ran to my bike, saw Guy still putting on his bike shorts, and took off on the twenty-five mile ride. I got caught up in a pack of five people. I knew that drafting, or riding so close behind someone else they blocked the wind for you was illegal.

• • •

The pack went a couple miles on the course and we went around a corner. A draft buster yelled out, 'Break it up.' I tried to go up in front. But after they passed the draft buster, they sped up and I was back in the pack again. When I finished the bike ride, I felt terrific.

"I jumped off my bike, put on my running shorts, and took off. Suddenly my legs felt awful and I couldn't make my hips turn over. I kept telling myself, 'Running is what you're best at. Run.' After two miles I loosened up and was all right."

When Joni crossed the finish line, she checked the board showing race times and thought that hers looked good. But she wouldn't know until later. She walked around to cool down, found Guy, who'd been looking for her, and had something to drink.

At the awards ceremony she listened intently when the announcer came to the forty to forty-four year-olds. He called out the fifth place woman and her time, then number four, three, and two. Joni looked at Guy.

When she heard her name as first place winner, she was stunned. The race had been sponsored by St. Anthony's Hospital and when a nun gave her a trophy, Joni couldn't let go of her hand. "Thank you. Thank you so much," Joni said.

To Joni, this win symbolized several personal victories with difficult choices. She had stepped away from her leisurely life-style, had worked out despite incredible pain, and had kept going in the face of fear and possible failure. But after winning her first triathlon, she felt sure she was choosing actions that were right for her.

◆ ◆ ◆

Her choices were helping her form a new definition of herself. As she learned and grew through her choices she became clearer about who she was. Each decision influenced the next one and each decision further defined who she was.

Joni didn't know then that her own choices—to build up her withered body, to practice and train, and to work toward becoming the best she could be—would ultimately affect others in a public way. She was making what she considered to be personal choices. And she continued making choices until the moment when there was no doubt, in her mind, that she was doing what she should be doing with her life.

As soon as she arrived home, Joni wanted to enter another triathlon. She chose the President's Triathlon in Dallas, Texas, because age group winners would be invited to the Ironman Triathlon in Hawaii.

In the spring of 1985, she flew to Dallas. When she saw her competition, many top women from California who'd trained all year, she didn't think she had a chance. But despite intense heat, she completed a one-and-a-half-mile swim in Lake Laverne, forty-two miles of bike riding around the lake, and a ten-mile run in three hours and fifty minutes—first again in her age group!

Joni was now eligible for the Ironman Triathlon, to be held in October. The sport shop owners urged her to get a coach and suggested Mark, a young man who had raced in the Ironman in 1983 and 1984, the same man she'd seen running in her neighborhood. Joni said she had to think about it. Rarely,

♦ ♦ ♦

if ever, had she missed an opportunity or a chance to move forward, but this next step raised concerns—training for the Ironman would take an enormous amount of time, she didn't want to be away from her family that much, and she didn't want to fail.

A month later, after easily winning a three-mile road race, Joni made her decision. She met Mark, who was clicking off times as runners finished. He encouraged her to enter the Ironman and agreed to supervise her training for the next five months.

"The next week he gave me a training schedule, with the focus on swimming and biking. He made out a list of the races he wanted me to enter. He wanted me to go into the Ironman as if it were just another day of training. I trusted him completely.

"After his own intense training for triathlons, he knew about nutrition, too. It didn't take long for him to realize my eating habits were terrible. I was drinking all this diet soda and I was a junk food freak. He wanted me on a complex carbohydrate diet, lots of grains, fruits, and vegetables. No red meat, chicken twice a month.

"Weight just fell off. My body had already changed because of training, but I began to see an amazing difference. With less body fat, my muscles were much more prominent.

"Mark and I spent a lot of time together and always had fun. He is sixteen years younger than I, but he'd had a lifetime of experiences and, in many ways, seemed a lot older.

"My training took time. On Saturdays and Sundays I'd leave the house at eight in the morning for a hundred-mile bike ride, a nine-mile run, and get home at six. At night I was tired but

◆ ◆ ◆

I looked forward to time with Bryan and Vaughn, who were both supportive of my training."

In October, Joni and Mark flew to Hawaii. On the morning of the race, they stood near the start of the swim area. Joni's body had been marked and she had on her goggles. "Just do the best job you can," Mark said. "That's all I want. I think you can make the top five of your age group. If not, that's okay. Just do your best."

As soon as the cannon boomed, over a thousand people ran into the water at once. The temperature of the ocean was so warm it felt like bath water. Joni could see fish swimming underneath her. She followed along the line of orange balls until she reached a large Polynesian boat that marked the first turn of the 2.4 mile swim. She swam around a second boat and headed for shore.

She got out of the water and saw that her time was 1:28. Ahead of schedule, she felt a rush of adrenaline. While running to the tent to change, she saw Mark, who looked at his watch and smiled.

Joni jumped on her bike and raced along miles of road, bordered by flat fields of porous black lava rock. Along the way race staff handed her water, guava jelly sandwiches, and cookies. Just before the 56-mile turnaround point, she felt winded as she peddled uphill for 7 miles.

"I couldn't ease up or I'd lose time. Near the end of the 112-mile course, I felt a surge of energy and went flying in. My time on my bike was 6 hours and 19 minutes."

As she changed into running shoes and shorts, Mark yelled, "Go for it. You're doing great! There are a few people ahead of you, but you can catch them."

That was what she needed to hear and ran for 6 miles.

♦ ♦ ♦

When she got to a steep hill going through a town, she slowed to a walk to rest. She was in so much pain she was beginning to think she couldn't go on. But out on the highway she made herself run again. At the 14-mile aid station, she stopped for water and sponged herself off. After walking for another 100 yards, she forced herself to run to the next aid station.

"I began an uphill climb and knew I had to conserve my energy if I was going to make the last 10 miles. I told myself I couldn't come this far and not finish. I had to turn my mind off and put one foot in front of the other."

When the sun set it became dark quickly. The runners were given light sticks to hook on the front of their shirts. The tubes, filled with a liquid that glowed, lit up the runners so that they could be seen by cars and other runners.

"It was mystical, unbelievable. I was overcome. I couldn't believe what it looked like. There were no sounds except feet on the pavement. As we got closer to aid stations we could hear cheering and yelling and that kept us moving. Then it faded until we got near the next one.

"When I had 1.7 miles to go, I was on the top of a high hill. I saw people lined up on both sides of the route and heard them screaming as runners crossed the line. It sounded so great that I started to fly and ran as if I were out sprinting. I was going so fast I ran past the Australian champion who'd won our age division last year. The previous record was 12:24, and when I crossed the finish line I glanced at the clock. It said 12:03.

"I'd won the women's masters division and set a new class record!

"I was filled with more self-confidence and respect for myself than I'd ever felt in my life. For the first time in my life,

◆ ◆ ◆

I felt I had accomplished something. I thought, this is just the beginning of what you're all about."

In that glorious moment Joni was aware of shifting. With her remarkable achievement came feelings of mastery and pleasure—a sense of well-being.

Well-being follows a shift. It may also follow a turning point, described by a woman in *Lifeprints* by Grace Baruch, Rosalind Barnett, and Caryl Rivers as "events that changed your life so that it is different afterward." Joni's win at the Ironman was just such a turning point.

A turning point in many ways resembles a positive shift, except that a shift need not occur as the result of an event. A shift's appearance can be quite subtle, merely a moment in which a change in attitude takes place. With either a shift or a turning point, there is change.

Shifting may seem like making a promise to ourselves. Those who have lived inside a promise know there is nothing comparable for confirming intentions.

Joni's intention to excel as a triathlete meant that no matter how forbidding or frightening certain aspects became there would be no space in her thinking for giving up. Whether training or in a race, she would persevere.

Even though Joni considered her triumph personal, she received coast to coast press. In 1985, catapulted into the sports limelight, she told interviewers relevant parts of her story. People heard that she was not stopped by barriers: when

♦ ♦ ♦

she felt pain, she took it with her and kept trying; when she felt fear, she took it with her and kept going.

The following year Joni competed in fourteen events. She raced in triathlons from the Endurance Ironman, for the national championship on Cape Cod, to the Ironman, for the world championship in Hawaii, where she defended her record.

But Joni's public acclaim was accompanied by a painful, private loss. When Vaughn once again asked her to stop competing so she could stay at home, she entered fewer races but couldn't abandon racing completely. Although Joni and Vaughn tried to resolve their conflicting needs, they finally divorced. Joni moved to a small apartment near the sports shop in town.

The next year, at age forty-six, she won her age group division in the President's Triathlon in Dallas, Texas, and became a member of the first U.S. National Triathlon Team. And in 1989 as well, she raced again at the Ironman and set another world-class record. In 1992, while competing in the first Olympic Distance World Championship, her intent is to promote goodwill, friendship, and world-class competition among triathletes around the world.

In addition to her public example, Joni also empowers others in a direct and personal way. "I'm coaching individual women, forty and over. One client, who's forty-one and has seven children aged thirteen to two, just did her first triathlon and can't wait until her next race. As the women I'm working with improve and their bodies change, I notice how they start to feel about themselves. It's exciting for me to see their self-esteem soar."

"I feel I'm giving back what was given to me. Other people

• • •

were role models for me. Because of them I made a discovery about myself—I didn't know there was a triathlete inside. Now I tell other people you don't know until you try—one reason I want to get my story out."

It had never occurred to Joni that she would become someone capable of mentoring. Now she recognizes that her own achievements are powerful enough to move others toward their goals. She accepts this responsibility by guiding middle-aged women to achieve their personal best. She seems to know instinctively the value of mentoring, that she cannot stop or depend on past trophies.

"I dread success," George Bernard Shaw once said. "To have succeeded is to have finished one's business on earth, like the male spider who is killed by the female the moment he has succeeded in his courtship. I like a state of continual becoming, with a goal in front and not behind."

Joni does, too. Out of her commitment to help others succeed, she is ensuring her future success.

Joni's interest in women athletes and masters has led her to take on projects at a national level. "Women in sports do not receive the recognition for their accomplishments that they should or that men do for the same event. I remember after one New York marathon, there were two or three photos of the male winner on the front page of the sports section with a full page of copy about how he felt all through the race. There were only three paragraphs on the female winner.

"I'm also working to get more recognition for masters,

♦ ♦ ♦

because competitors over forty really are role models. During events like the Ironman there could be a television camera on the lead man and woman. Audiences should be aware of who they are and what they've done.

"Masters can be an inspiration to people watching in arm chairs, thinking they're too old. I believe it's never too late to become healthy, to get in shape, and to make that a way of life."

MARIE

♦ ♦ ♦

"It makes me feel wonderful to remember how each woman came into our halfway house—scared and frightened—and then to see the calmness and serenity of sobriety."

8

On a cold, windy January morning I was on my way to Shepherd House, a halfway house for women with drug and alcohol problems, to meet Marie. Marie was both cofounder and director of the house.

After stepping off the subway onto an outdoor platform at Savin Hill in Dorchester, just south of Boston, I pulled up the collar of my trenchcoat, rushed up a damp cement stairway, and stood on the sidewalk in a patch of sunlight for warmth.

• • •

While I waited for Marie's secretary to pick me up, I tried to get a sense of this neighborhood, similar to the one Marie had grown up in and lived in while she was married.

Across the way, in the window of the Bulldogs Tavern, a Schlitz sign flashed on and off. Local residents carried bags of groceries out of Murphy's Shamrock Supermarket and bags of laundry into the Savvy Professional Cleaners and Laundromat. Triple-decker houses, painted peach, green, blue, and yellow, bordered both sides of the street.

From telephone conversations with Marie, I already knew some things about her. In addition to an alcohol problem, she'd been addicted to prescription pills. At age twenty-one she'd married her high school sweetheart and they'd had nine children.

A car horn honked. The strawberry blonde driver of a black Buick leaned toward me and waved. I slid into the passenger seat beside her. "I'm Thelma," she said, "Marie's assistant." Thelma told me that two years ago she had been a resident at Shepherd House. "Marie saved my life," she said.

We drove up Jones Hill, looking at turrets, cupolas, and lacy gingerbread embellishments on large Victorian houses. At the crest of the hill we faced the hazy, slate blue buildings of Boston in the distance. Thelma slowed the car to a stop in front of a large, brown, shingled house.

A small woman in a gray wool suit ran down the steps to greet me. Marie took both my hands in hers, looked into my eyes, then hugged me. Her black hair, just turning gray, curled softly around her face. She was in her midfifties but looked closer to forty.

I followed her up the wooden steps into the front hall of the house. Oak paneling made the hallway seem dark, but it felt light and warm with the sound of women's voices and laughter coming from the living room—a seminar in progress.

Upstairs, as Marie showed me some of the bedrooms she had decorated with matching chintz spreads and ruffled curtains, she told me about several residents: a pediatrician's daughter, a prostitute, a nurse addicted to Valium, an older divorced woman who'd been living alone, a young woman whose father owned a chain of Chinese restaurants, and the twenty-year-old daughter of a dentist who didn't think his daughter had a problem.

In her office, above shelves of resource books, I noticed a citation from the City of Boston. There was a framed article: "Marie Conroy earned her status as South Shore Woman of the Year the hard way." A *Boston Globe* headline read, SHE'S BEEN THERE, SHE KNOWS: FOR WOMEN ALCOHOLICS, A PLACE TO TURN TO.

We sat down on a comfortable white sofa, and Marie began her story.

In a white-washed two-room cottage near the village of Fermanagh in Northern Ireland, six-year-old Mary Ellen lived happily with four brothers and three sisters. She planted potatoes and fed the chickens with her father. She baked bread and made clothes with her mother.

Then suddenly Mary Ellen's mother died while giving birth to her ninth baby. A few weeks later relatives, Ellen and Tom from the United States, arrived at their cottage and offered to take Mary Ellen home with them.

"I didn't want to go far away with strangers. I wanted to stay with my father and brothers and sisters. But I guess they

◆ ◆ ◆

thought it would be a relief for my father to have one less child to take care of. Ellen was forty-five and had no children. She brought me an orange knit dress with a brown and white polka-dot tie to wear on my trip to America."

Mary Ellen went to live with Ellen and Tom on the top floor of a brown, triple-decker house in Dorchester. They enrolled her in St. Peter's, a neighborhood parochial school. Mary Ellen was confused by new words and American ways of doing things. Amused by her, the nuns and priests sat her on their desks in front of classrooms so that the children could look at her large, brown eyes, short black hair and bangs, and listen to her Irish brogue.

A few months later Ellen and Tom renamed her Marie. Then they adopted her and changed her last name, too—she became Marie Maguire. She missed her family in Ireland but heard nothing from them.

"I needed to feel wanted by someone and so I did everything Ellen asked me to do. She was a large, stern woman with her hair pulled tightly into a bun behind her head. I did all the cleaning. She sat in a chair watching while I dusted around the circles and carved places on the piano. Then I had to sit on the back porch and read my catechism over and over. If I said a wrong word or did anything she didn't like, I was sent to my room.

"I was miserable and lonesome but wasn't allowed to say anything or ask any questions. I had feelings inside I wanted to come out, but she shut me down. I always tried to smile and be happy so they would like me.

"Tom was kind. People said he looked like President Roosevelt. Whenever Ellen went out, he and I talked and laughed. Maybe he was afraid of her, too.

◆ ◆ ◆

"When I was fourteen Tom died. I felt so alone without him. I couldn't believe he died and left me with Ellen.

"That year I'd met a boy I liked, Jim. I'd seen him working in the First National supermarket. He was seventeen, a short, stocky, dark-haired Irish boy. I thought he was the cutest thing and so smart. And when Tom died, Jim came to the wake.

"Right after the wake Ellen turned on me. I couldn't understand it, but she blamed me for her husband's death. I almost believed her, but then I thought, no, I liked Tom and he liked me."

Ellen began to drink heavily—one can of beer after the other and from an open bottle of whiskey she kept on the kitchen table. She shouted at Marie and refused to let her go out with friends.

"I wanted to get away from her and see my friends, but I felt so guilty if I went out and left her. She was the only family I had. I felt responsible for her and sorry for her because she was alone.

"One night, when I was sixteen, she said I could go out if I came back by nine o'clock. At eight forty-five I got up to the top floor of the house, but couldn't get in. The door was locked. I knew she was inside drinking. I was so afraid she'd be angry if I were late that I put my fist through the glass, reached in, and tried to open the door. But she had nailed it shut. I sat down on the steps and cried. Two hours later, she came to the door and let me in."

For ten years, Marie didn't hear from anyone in her family. She wondered why her family hadn't wanted her, why they couldn't have brought up one more child. Finally she got an address and wrote to her father. Her older brother Seamus

♦ ♦ ♦

sent a letter saying that he was coming to Boston to see her. Marie was overjoyed.

"Seamus wasn't in that house two days and right away he said, 'I can't believe you're living this way.' He couldn't take Ellen's drinking and yelling. He moved into a rooming house nearby. I put up with her because I had no one else."

When Marie turned eighteen and finished high school she wanted to marry Jim. But he thought she was still too young and he wanted to go into the marines. So she worked at the telephone company and went out with other young men. They treated her kindly, took her to dances, and out for dinner.

"But whenever Jim came home on leave I always wanted to see him. Sometimes he was attentive, other times he ignored me. I rationalized that he had his family and five brothers and sisters to attend to. Even though I felt last in importance to him, I didn't question it then.

"Finally Jim got out of the service. He didn't finish his senior year at Boston College and took a job at the post office. I was still working at the telephone company. When we got together, we planned to have our wedding in two years and started saving.

"On my way down the aisle of St. Peter's Church, with my brother Seamus giving me away, I thought at last I would be happy. I'd have someone to care for me."

"I felt such guilt for leaving Ellen. There were nights when it would rain or snow and I'd be lying in bed with Jim asleep beside me, listening to the wind. Wind brought back my sadness as a child. And I'd be thinking, I shouldn't

♦ ♦ ♦

be doing this. I shouldn't be married to this man. I shouldn't have left her."

While Marie struggled with her ambivalence about leaving Ellen, she tried hard to please Jim. Nine months after their marriage she had her first baby, Mike. Fourteen months later Jane was born. During the next several years, she had a baby nearly every year, until there were nine children.

As their family grew Jim's and Marie's relationship changed. Jim began to doubt Marie's love for him. She often heard him telling his friends that they should never marry a pretty lady. He began to insult her; he told her that her nose was too big. Marie hid her feelings.

"I felt unsure of him. He got angry if any other man looked at me. But I had eyes for no one but Jim. I still thought he was the only one who would love me."

After they had been married five years, Marie had her first drink. "I liked what alcohol did for me. Drinks made me feel good, pretty, and confident. At a New Year's Eve party my husband saw me dancing and got so mad he left the party. I was so afraid of being left behind, I followed him home. But he wouldn't talk to me.

"I told him, 'I won't dance with anyone else again.' I told him how much I loved him. I begged him to tell me he loved me. But he pushed me away.

"I discovered that if Jim and I had a few drinks, he would be more romantic and loving. And drinks let me become the happy person I wanted to be. We became drinking buddies. But when I wasn't drinking, I didn't know how to talk to him or how to please him.

"He wanted a woman to be sweet and adorable, up on a pedestal and perfect, like his mother. She kept her house just

♦ ♦ ♦

so and had her children air out their rooms for three hours on Saturday mornings before they made their beds. Jim liked it when I wore an apron and worked all day, cooking, cleaning, doing the wash, and taking care of the babies and children."

At the same time Marie continued to care for Ellen, who was drinking more and visiting more, usually with a pint in her purse. "She'd come in and sit at the kitchen table and say, 'Have a little drink. My God, you've got to make dinner for all those kids. How can you stand all those kids without a drink?'

"I started to have a drink before supper when I was working alone in the kitchen. When I served supper I always wanted to be sure Jim was happy with it. I'd wring my hands and say to him, 'Do you like the supper? Do you like it?' I'd be so glad if he nodded.

"I knew I was a hard worker, but I didn't take pride in what I did. As soon as I finished one job, like making a good supper, instead of feeling good about it I'd think of ways I could have made it better. And I always thought I should accomplish more. When my housework was done I thought I should be sewing. I could never relax or feel satisfied with anything I did.

"I was always in the background. Jim used to take 'his boys,' he called them, to the L Street Beach bathhouse to show them off. Before they ever left the house I had to put every one of them into the bathtub because he wanted them spotless. He'd leave with 'his boys,' and his little girl, Jane, would be sitting alone on the stairs.

"Jim wanted the whole family to go off on day trips and picnics. You know—you take the high chair; you take the playpen; you take the cooler. When we'd come home he'd drop me and all those hot, sweaty, sandy kids off with the buckets of leftover food. He'd come into the kitchen and say, 'I'll be right back.' And, of course, he'd go out to get a cool one. And I'd have to clean up the kids, the mess, and get dinner ready with no help from him ever. I did it time and time again."

"The babies kept coming. There was a lot I couldn't keep up with, and it was getting harder to manage. I needed more energy. Even though I weighed only one hundred and three pounds, a doctor put me on diet pills. They were marvelous. Oh, my God, I thought, they're the answer. They helped me keep going and do it all.

"I'd started to drink heavily at home, but no one really knew. We didn't have company and we didn't go out, except to the children's schools. Jim worked two jobs—the post office during the day and the supermarket at night.

"Many nights I'd drink too much and forget to fix Jane's dress for the school play or to correct Jimmy's math homework. And when I woke up in the morning and realized all the promises I'd broken, I'd say, 'Oh, no, I did it again.'

"Jim was drinking heavily, too. He'd go to a bar, come home drunk, and shout and hit me. He accused me of seeing other men and called me a whore. I cried night after night trying to defend myself.

"One night he went into the kitchen to throw out some beer cans and saw a few dishes in the sink. 'This place's a mess!" he shouted.

"Now Jim was a very strong man, a handball player who'd won many tournaments, but I was so angry I threw the first

◆ ◆ ◆

punch. He threw the second. He yanked and ripped my dress. I called the police. When Station Eleven came down, my dress was hanging off, my slip was showing, and my hair was a mess. Jim was sitting calmly in a chair, so the police took me out. I called back, 'Him! It's what he's doing to me!' "

Despite her protests, the police put Marie into the paddy wagon and took her to city hospital. Although X rays showed no broken bones, she was kept overnight.

"In the early morning hours I took a bus home. When I got to my back door the children were on their way out to school. With their heads bowed down, they walked right past me.

"I felt so much shame, guilt, and remorse. How could I live with that? The only way I knew was to go out as soon as the package store opened and get a bottle of vodka.

"Yet I was a person who thought you should have dignity in front of your neighbors. Nobody should know you're fighting, even though the paddy wagon is coming to your house in the middle of the night. I'd walk out the next day pushing two kids in a carriage, two beside the carriage, and I'd have a bottle under the baby's mattress. I thought nobody knew."

A year later Marie had her eighth baby, a boy with a critically damaged heart. She often took him to Children's Hospital in the morning and didn't return home until late in the afternoon.

"And there'd be seven kids waiting for me. My God, a child with heart problems. I used it as another reason to drink.

"On Christmas Eve that year Jim and I drank while we wrapped the children's presents. By late that night we didn't care how the gifts looked and just tossed them under the tree. On Christmas Day the children's friends came over to the house to look at their gifts, and one child brought his new Polaroid camera. My son Jimmy said, 'Hey, take a picture of my mother.'

"There I was in my late twenties, but I looked fifty. My apron on, my stockings rolled to below my knees, and a beer on the floor beside me. How sad for my kids.

"Jim and I grew further apart. We were both drinking, but not together anymore. We were just drinking to cope. I'd say to myself, 'What's happening to us? We started out as decent people.'

"The thought, at that time, of divorce or separation—I mean, how could I? I was nearly thirty; I still loved Jim; I had eight kids; and I needed income to take care of those kids. I didn't have experience to do anything else, and I was drinking.

"A few times I tried to talk to Jim about how I felt, but it always ended in an argument. I was so insecure, so afraid of abandonment, that I'd make up. I was always sorry. All my life I thought I was wrong."

In her late twenties, Marie had her own problems as well as Ellen's. In her mid-seventies, living alone, and drinking alcoholically, Ellen was hospitalized often for her heart and "acute gastritis," an alcohol-related condition.

"Even with all the kids and housework, my mind was always on her. I'd get a call and I'd go right over there. Sometimes I wouldn't hear from her for a week or two. Then she'd come to my house, and I'd have her sleep on the couch. I never showed my anger or mentioned her drinking.

"One night Ellen didn't answer my calls. I found her sitting in a chair, holding the phone. She was dead.

♦ ♦ ♦

"I was in shock about her death and about her apartment. It was booze bottles from one end to the other. I was questioned by the police. And I had a hard time getting through her wake. But no one knew how empty I felt.

"After the wake, while I walked baby John on the beach in South Boston, I felt sick. I knew it was from the alcohol. When I got home, I put the baby and the other children to bed and sat down to write out the thank-you cards for masses.

"Suddenly my head seemed to split open. I'd been so tired but didn't let anyone know, not even Jim. He thought I was Superwoman. I did, too. God forbid that I should be human, have feelings, faults, pain, and sadness, loneliness, despair, and time off. I didn't know I had a right to all those things.

"I vaguely remember going into the hospital, where they put me into the psychiatric ward. The next thing I knew I was sitting on a long bench in a hospital johnny looking at other patients sitting beside me. One was a young seminarian who'd overworked, another was a student. I was saying to myself, 'Oh God, look how sick they are.'

"Of course I was sick, too. The staff didn't know what was wrong, but I knew it was the drinking. The doctors didn't look at my drinking or ask what pills I was taking. They didn't talk about how many kids I had or wonder how I was coping. All they knew was that Ellen had died.

"They thought I needed shock treatments. I knew I wasn't mentally ill. I was depressed. After a treatment I was a quiet little mouse. They gave me sixteen treatments, and I lost my memory."

After two months Marie's doctor said she could go home for a weekend. "I couldn't wait to see the children. They gave me something no one else did. I needed them more than they

♦ ♦ ♦

needed me. I just loved to hold their hands in mine. On the way home from the hospital Jim drove me around to all the relative's houses and we picked up the kids. It was a good reunion. And at the end of the weekend I refused to go back to the hospital."

A few days later a neighbor who liked to drink brought over a bottle of wine. Marie hadn't had a drink for two months. The women sat at the kitchen table talking and drinking, until Marie passed out on the kitchen floor.

"That wine started me drinking again, and I couldn't stop for another four years. Both Jim and I drank heavily. Those were the worst years of my life.

"One night, after I'd been drinking and Jim had come home drunk and gone to bed, I took out paint cans and brushes to paint the bedroom. I'd seen a purple canopylike thing in a woman's magazine and wanted our bedroom to look like that. I splashed purple paint on the bed Jim was sleeping in and on the walls behind him. He woke up and lay there watching me. I knew he was thinking I was crazy."

Not yet ready to see her own problems that clearly, Marie went to work on Jim's drinking. She called a neighbor, Jerry, a recovering alcoholic, and asked him to help Jim.

"Jerry knew I needed help, too, so when he arrived he offered to take us both to a self-help meeting. I said I was okay, it was Jim who needed the help. When they walked out the door I said, 'Beautiful,' and poured myself a drink.

"But the next time I went. In the meeting hall I looked around at all the faces. I liked what I saw. There were so

♦ ♦ ♦

many happy people, laughing and talking. I wondered if I could ever feel that way."

After attending a few more meetings, Marie stopped drinking. Jim, however, stopped going to meetings and continued to drink. She recalled the early days of their marriage and how drinking had brought them closer, how kind Jim had been.

"One clear October night we sat out on the porch together. Although I felt marvelous not drinking, I wanted to be close to my husband. I felt bad that I wasn't his drinking buddy anymore. It had been several months since I'd had a drink, and I thought that, well, maybe, I could drink again. Maybe I was different now. Maybe I wasn't really an alcoholic."

Marie glanced at Jim, went inside to the refrigerator, and came back with a can of beer. That one beer set up a physical craving and a mental obsession with alcohol that started her drinking again.

"My drinking got even worse that time. Sometimes I'd wake up in the morning and couldn't remember if I'd fed the kids. I felt such guilt. They'd plead with me not to drink, but I couldn't stop. I hated myself."

Three months later something happened. It was not a big event, just a quiet realization. On New Year's Eve they went to a party at a neighbor's and had too much to drink.

"When I woke up in the morning I knew. I just knew. That was enough. I knew I didn't have to drink again. I remember saying to myself, 'You've got strengths and you can't let them die.' There was a fire inside me that I didn't want to go out. I didn't know how I was going to cope or face the future without drinking or whether I could stop if Jim kept on, but I had to try."

♦ ♦ ♦

For Marie there were so many complicating factors that it seemed unlikely she would come to the point of accepting her addiction to alcohol and pills.

As with most addicts who suffer guilt and remorse, Marie's self-value was low. Her low self-value had begun when she was deserted, physically and emotionally, by her family. From then on she lived with a fear of being abandoned again.

A frightened, insecure little girl, Marie's basic needs for affirmation and security went unfilled. While being raised by a controlling alcoholic woman, Marie endured treatment that to an outsider would have seemed intolerable or unacceptable. She had never learned what "normal" was, a phenomenon common among children who grew up in alcoholic homes and those raised in dysfunctional families. From her early years, she received some mixed-up messages. Through no fault of her own, Marie grew up equating love with rejection, not knowing how to have an intimate relationship, and learning to be loyal in circumstances where her loyalty was not deserved.

Because she was an untreated adult child of an alcoholic, Marie had few resources for recognizing that what was going on in her own home was not normal. Jim couldn't help her because he, too, had been raised in an alcoholic family. When his drinking became alcoholic and his behavior erratic, Marie's tendency was to adjust and put up with it. It was an easy next step for her to become a codependent—more concerned about Jim's addiction than her own.

In addition, addictions are so powerful they cause people

♦ ♦ ♦

to build up equally powerful defenses to avoid having to acknowledge or deal with them. Denial, of course, is integral to addiction, as strong in the beginning of addictive behavior as it is at the end. It was natural for Marie to hide in her addictions and to rationalize her use of alcohol and pills.

Denial and low self-value extinguished any desire Marie might have had to help herself. Instead, her energy and concern were for Jim. She tried to be the perfect wife and mother to please him, even to drink with him if that would make them closer.

With so much conflict and denial swirling within, it seemed a miracle that Marie could identify the "fire" she didn't want to go out. Feeling her "strengths" indicated a flicker, deep inside. That spark of self-value was just enough to bring her to acceptance.

"I went to more meetings with Jerry and other members of the group and made new friends. My new women friends called me every day. And I couldn't wait to see them at night for another meeting.

"Right away I began to feel better. I looked better, and for the first time I felt hope. I felt good because I could hold my kids in my arms and I started to feel my feelings. You know when you're drinking you can't really feel love and you can't give it.

"I felt loving toward Jim, but he didn't adjust very well to my sobriety and tried everything to keep me from going to meetings. One night before I left, he hurled an eighty-year-old Irish crystal pitcher that had come from my family into

♦ ♦ ♦

the kitchen sink. It was the only material thing I had that meant something to me. I put all the pieces into a black velvet bag and carried it around with me for months. It was like a smashed dream. But I didn't drink over it.

"I took not drinking one day at a time. And I realized from the people I was meeting that I wasn't worthless."

As she started to feel better about who she was, Marie began to experience the rewards of networking. She was getting support from men and women who were also recovering alcoholics on a one-to-one basis as well as from her participation in several groups. The people who'd been successful achieving sobriety served as her empowering examples.

The power of groups to heal individuals has become recognized. "It has become increasingly evident that cooperation for survival among members of the same species is a basic law of life," Dr. van der Kolk writes in *Psychological Trauma.* "Throughout the history of man, sharing relationships has been the central mode of coping with and adapting to the environment."

At group discussions, Marie heard that she wasn't alone. Her group work gave her a sense of belonging, a healthy interdependence on others. When she talked about her pain and guilt, she learned how her disease had affected her and those around her. Gradually she felt better about herself; her self-value improved; and she was able to take steps to make peace with her past.

Fannie Flagg, an actress and author who benefitted from

♦ ♦ ♦

group support, wrote in *Lears,* "Though all of us may have some family and friends, we can't reveal as much of ourselves to them as we can in group settings. This is because people in groups aren't judgmental or emotionally involved with us, and they have a much clearer understanding of our problems because they've been there themselves and can relate to our stories."

"The happier I was, the more it seemed like Jim just couldn't stand me. He hated the fact that I had now become a stronger person. Whenever he drank he looked for a fight. He ripped the telephone off the wall. He pulled up the banister and threw it down the stairs. He slapped me and bruised my face. One time he hit me so hard, he broke my nose.

"Even though I'd stopped drinking, I still didn't feel enough self-worth to tell him I'd had enough. Once I did pack my bags and went by bus to Cape Cod to see a cousin, but I came right back. I kept putting up with Jim because of my fears. And he was a charmer. He'd say, 'I'm sorry' and 'I love you.' And I'd say, 'Okay.' "

The next year, when she was thirty-five, Marie had her ninth baby, a second girl. Her older daughter, Jane, was eleven and called herself Midget Mother. She helped Marie with the baby and they folded laundry together for two to three hours every afternoon.

"I hadn't had a drink for four years. I was relating well to the children and wanted to keep the marriage going. Jim finally saw that his problem with alcohol was interfering with our marriage and his relationships with the kids, and he went into a detox. He didn't drink for a while and things were much better between us."

The next year her brothers and sisters invited Marie and Jim to visit Ireland. Although her father had died three years before, Marie wanted to see the rest of her family. It had been thirty-four years. And she hoped the trip would strengthen her marriage.

"My sister Susan met us at Shannon airport. I was so happy to see my brothers and sisters, their houses, and Ireland. It was good to meet their children, my nieces and nephews, and to see the cottage where I'd been born.

"I looked into my sisters' faces, and for the first time I realized who I was. Before I'd thought I had potential, but after that I knew I had strengths. I saw that my children also looked like my family—all my life I'd thought these were my husband's kids. Knowing my family made me feel good about myself. From then on I grew. I got the confidence and strength I needed to do what I had to do."

During the visit she learned that there was alcoholism in her family. For the three-week stay in Ireland, Jim didn't drink. But Marie knew he was having a very tough time.

The day they returned to Boston he started drinking again. He compared Marie to her sisters. "They're so wonderful! Why aren't you?"

A month later Jane was so upset by her father's drinking, she quietly told her mother that she couldn't stand having any more nightmares. As Marie hugged her daughter she said to herself, "This young woman has gone through enough. Her brothers, too. There are too many indignities. No human being deserves this."

• • •

"The next day I asked Jim to leave. That was the beginning of my life."

Strengthened by the affirmation and empowering examples she discovered in her own family, Marie recognized more choices. She shed her shabby view of herself and her submissive role of victim, choosing to be a functional, healthy woman and mother.

For Marie these choices took courage. Her choices meant breaking old patterns of enabling, overcoming her fears, and moving past shame and blame to respect for herself.

Marie's intention to make difficult decisions had, at first, been thwarted by Jim. Threatened by the different dynamic in their marriage and by his wife's growing independence, he had resisted her changes. "We will see how it is that those closest to us often have the greatest investment in our staying the same," Harriet Lerner wrote in *The Dance of Anger,* "despite whatever criticisms and complaints they may openly voice. We also resist the very changes that we seek. This resistance to change, like the will to change, is a natural and universal aspect of all human systems."

It was as hard for Marie to make the choice to recover from her addictions in the face of Jim's resistance as it was for her to overcome her belief that she might be to blame for her failed marriage and, therefore, ought to stay.

Like Marie, we might continue to be attracted to a partner who puts us down or criticizes us, but for whom we still feel some sympathy. It might be worth considering what keeps us in that relationship, why we stay. Could it be that we linger because we believe the conflict is our fault?

◆ ◆ ◆

"For a woman, even to feel conflict with anyone, and particularly but not only with men," Jean Baker Miller writes in *Toward a New Psychology of Women,* "has meant that something is wrong with her 'psychologically' since one is supposed to 'get along' if one is 'all right.' The initial sensing of conflict then becomes an almost immediate proof that she is wrong and moreover 'abnormal.' Some of women's best impulses and sources of energy are thus nipped in the bud."

Marie's talents and energies were indeed stifled for a number of years. But in sobriety she was coming to respect herself, learning to make beneficial choices, and preparing herself to make more.

"Right away I got a job at the Bickford Pancake House, working nights until two or three in the morning. I was the floor manager, the hostess, and I did the register. I didn't know the business, but a nice older man helped me and I caught on quickly. I'd always been a worker, so work wasn't a problem for me.

"Jim and I got a legal separation, although I hoped he would stop drinking and we could get back together. He went to live in the three-family house we still owned in South Boston and gave me the single family house we'd been living in, in Dorchester.

"Jane was sixteen and took care of the younger kids who were five to fifteen. I saw that they went to school. I felt good because we were growing together. The kids saw my recovery, that I was okay, that I wasn't as nervous.

"I finally felt I was a person in my own right and knew I was capable of terrific things."

♦ ♦ ♦

Marie's changed outlook, discarded habits, and fresh confidence signaled that she had come to the shifting stage of self-empowerment. Sure of herself and her ability to make it on her own, Marie knew that nothing—not people or events—could impede her progress.

Marie's shift can be compared to author Edward Fitzgerald's new approach, described in *That Place in Minnesota.* His "worst moment" after stopping drinking happened on a flight from Montreal to New York that took twelve hours. "Three airplanes were cancelled from under me by the snow, one after I'd sat in it on the runway for three hours, and when everybody rushed for a drink, I took a deep breath and had a Coca-Cola. When they finally opened up La Guardia and they were able to sneak us in from Boston, I felt good. I was going home late but I was going home sober."

Like Fitzgerald, Marie felt a similar relief and gratitude that she had reached another level, a different way of coping. She had redefined herself, putting her energies, direction, and intentions into clear, sharp focus.

While Marie was gaining mastery over her own circumstances, she had been helping friends and neighbors with drinking problems begin their own journeys back to health. Marie had done so well that when Action for Boston Community Development (ABCD) announced a need for alcoholism counselors to staff regional offices, a friend submitted her name.

When Marie went in for her interview, she was "scared

stiff." Her only outside work experience had been in a restaurant and her only counseling experience had been informal. "I couldn't believe it when they chose me over four men and gave me a scholarship to the Rutgers Institute for Alcoholism Studies in New Jersey. I spent the next year away, living in a dorm and coming home on weekends to see the kids, buy the food, and do the wash. Jane and the older kids were in charge during the week. Sunday nights I'd go back and meet my friends who'd gone into New York City for the weekend. Honest to God, I never envied them.

"I hadn't gone further than high school, but there I was, at forty, taking courses in counseling skills, writing, coordinating services, and the nature of alcoholism. I learned about the Jellenik theory—that people with a drinking problem didn't have to 'hit bottom' before deciding to stop. It was possible for alcoholics to stop drinking while they were still employed, married, and the car was intact."

None of the classes were easy for Marie. She was hesitant to speak up during discussions, afraid her comments would be wrong. An instructor advised that if she had something to say, to say it—if it was wrong, it was wrong. After that Marie became more assertive.

When she received her certification as a licensed social worker, she began working in the courts for ABCD. The courts referred people with drug and alcohol problems to her.

"I started to wonder where women alcoholics could go at night. In the early seventies, women alcoholics were considered unfit for society. Most of the men had someone to take care of them, but the women didn't. I worried about the woman alcoholic who would be on the streets of Boston, who'd gone

♦ ♦ ♦

from man to man. She needed help for her drinking, someone who would really care about her, and a place to live.

"I met other women, women who had once come from good backgrounds, but they were women nobody wanted anymore. I'd ask, 'Where are you staying tonight?' 'I don't know,' they'd say. These women were homeless.

"Self-help groups were important. But if you didn't have a warm bed, and you didn't have a good meal, and you didn't have a place to go after a meeting, how were you going to get anything from that meeting?"

Then Marie met James Yetman, a social worker who worked at a rehab center and halfway house for men. She told him that she wanted to start a halfway house for women. He didn't know if women would admit to a drinking problem or go to a home, but he agreed to help.

They began by going to Station Eleven, the same station that had sent paddy wagons to Marie's house years before, to ask if the police knew of a place suitable for use as a halfway house. At first the police discouraged their idea, but then suggested an empty house on Jones Hill. It had five bedrooms and a large dormitorylike room on the third floor.

Marie and James each put down $1,000, borrowed $10,000 from a bank, and bought the house for $12,000. They went to the Department of Public Health, Division of Alcoholism, and told them what they wanted to do, hired a lawyer, and made arrangements to incorporate.

"After seeing the lawyer, we were driving along and I said, 'What will we call the house?' We thought about the area we were in and considered Jones Hill Inn. But then I said, 'What we're doing is looking after people, so how about Shepherd House?' Jim agreed."

♦ ♦ ♦

For months they worked until late at night getting the house ready. City Hospital gave them fourteen beds and their friends made curtains and painted. Marie and James used their own money for initial expenses. They had no state funding yet and could not get foundation support until they had proved themselves.

In 1974, the week before Easter, the first woman arrived at their door. Her face was badly bruised and swollen. At the end of the week Marie took her home for Easter dinner. But two days later the man who had beaten her called and, in five minutes, she went back to him.

From that experience Marie recognized the insidiousness of a destructive relationship and looked hard at her own marriage. They were still legally separated. Her husband was still drinking and trying to undermine her professional efforts. Marie gave up hope of a reconciliation and asked him for a divorce.

A few months later, she moved to a modern house in a town south of Boston. She continued to work at ABCD during the day and to volunteer at Shepherd House at night. The following year, as more women paid to go into the house, Marie was able to pay herself a small salary and work there full-time.

The previous year laws regarding alcoholism had changed. Alcoholism was no longer considered a crime but recognized as a disease. And only a year after Shepherd House opened the city of Boston commended Marie and James for their "success by demonstrating empathy and understanding to the victims of the disease of alcoholism. . . ." The citation urged them to continue their work and contribution to the citizens of Boston.

♦ ♦ ♦

In addition to working with the women at Shepherd House, Marie gave presentations on the recovery process for women at high schools, colleges, and medical schools. When she spoke Marie knew that she had become a role model and often included parts of her story.

At Shepherd House Marie set up schedules and programs. "Each day the women have to be up, fully dressed, and downstairs for breakfast by eight-thirty. The day begins with meditation and exercise.

"Group work is very important. That's where they get confronted by each other, and that's where they get feedback. On Friday nights we have a sexuality group and talk about promiscuity, women's issues, and feelings. We teach fifteen-year-olds and fifty-year-olds. The women could be nurses, stewardesses, or prostitutes. The older ones think they know everything, so I have to say, 'We're not talking about sex. We're talking about you as a sexual person, which you have been since the day you were born.'

"The women go to self-help meetings held in the house and at nearby churches. They start to feel good about themselves and to get feelings of self-worth.

"After six weeks of state or private funding, each woman is expected to get a full-time job and pay for room and board. If they don't want to return to their old jobs, they have to get out the Sunday paper and look for jobs. It's a program of responsibility, but responsibility with freedom. And they are free to leave any time.

"At five months we begin to talk about termination, their responsibility for themselves, and their fears. Before they leave sometimes their anxiety is as acute as the day they came in.

• • •

They're leaving people who have become family. They'll be living a new life, without alcohol and drugs. Some residents live together. Most live nearby.

"When I see them again I'm so proud," Marie said, standing up and walking to her office window. This was our fourth session together. She turned around and smiled. "It makes me feel wonderful to remember how each woman came into our halfway house, scared and frightened, and then to see the calmness and serenity of sobriety."

Through mentoring, Marie had given the priceless gift of a second chance to hundreds of individual women. And in the process she had become a fully productive, highly respected member of her community and a woman who had achieved twenty-seven years of sobriety.

Marie felt comfortable fostering the growth of others. But with her history of codependency and caretaking, it had taken enormous growth on her part to learn the difference between supporting the residents in their recovery and assuming too much caretaking responsibility for them.

Harriet Lerner clarifies this distinction for women in *The Dance of Anger.* "Women have gained both identity and esteem from our deep investment in protecting, helping, nurturing, and comforting others," she wrote. "The problem arises when we are excessively reactive to other people's problems, when we assume responsibility for things that we are not responsible for, and when we attempt to control things that are not in our control. When we overfunction for another individual, we end

♦ ♦ ♦

up very angry, and in the process, we facilitate the growth of no one."

Marie took her final step away from overfunctioning when she decided to divorce. She turned to working further on her own recovery. Her growth led to an interest and concern for others who were going through what she had. Her desire to help others recover from addictions was a healthy one.

And it was natural for Marie to want to be connected to other people in a loving way. In *Necessary Losses* Judith Viorst, writes about a woman's "wish to be part of a web of human relationships, a wish not only to get—but to give—loving care. To need other people to help and console you, to share the good times and bad, to say 'I understand,' to be on your side—and also to need the reverse, to need to be needed—may lie at the heart of a woman's very identity." It does lie at the heart of mentoring and describes accurately the reciprocal supportive interaction of self-empowerment.

Jean Baker Miller refers to one facet of this interaction as "active participation in the development of others." In *Toward a New Psychology of Women* she discusses the ways women build other people's psychological resources, often characterized by such words as "mothering," "nurturing," and "caretaking." "Another way to describe this activity," Miller wrote, "is to say that women try to use their powers, that is, their intellectual and emotional abilities, to empower others, to build other people's strengths, resources, effectiveness, and well-being. . . . No one grows at all without these kinds of interactions."

Marie knew them well. Her skills have helped fourteen hundred women.

♦ ♦ ♦

In October of 1990 Marie retired and was honored at a dinner party held at the Kennedy Library in South Boston. Nearly all of the fourteen hundred women she had helped, and their families, attended. The public health commissioner spoke: "You've touched and changed so many lives." He presented Marie with a Certificate of Appreciation from the commonwealth of Massachusetts "for sixteen years of service as a pioneer of women's services." From the city of Boston she was awarded a resolution for attending to the needs of those suffering from alcohol and substance abuse. A former resident spoke for many when she said from the podium to Marie, sitting in a wing chair on stage, "You've given love to us so fully and unconditionally. If it weren't for you and Shepherd House being there, I wouldn't be here today."

ELIZABETH ROSE

♦ ♦ ♦

"Disease is an opportunity to learn to love yourself."

9

"I've had so much horrible abuse all my life," forty-five-year-old Elizabeth Rose said. "First my father, who terrorized me and my entire family. Then my husband, who tormented me by bringing home other men and women for sex.

"From all this stress, my immune system shattered. I was diagnosed with environmental illness, which meant that hundreds of substances in the environment had become toxic to me. Nearly everything made me sick, some things sent me into shock. I was at death's door many times."

◆ ◆ ◆

Elizabeth Rose was telling me her story at a deserted lunch table in the ballroom of the Ambassador Hotel in Los Angeles. We began talking shortly after I'd finished speaking at the Book and Author Lunch about women whose lives exemplified personal courage. She was one of many women who'd come to the podium to share their experiences.

A tall, glamorous, chestnut-haired woman wearing scarlet red, Elizabeth Rose had stood out. In a soft yet commanding voice, she'd said, "I've overcome child abuse, sexual abuse, poverty, eating disorders, divorce, and breakdown of my immune system. Now I'm helping other people. I'd like to be in your next book to tell others how I survived."

I had stayed at the podium awhile longer because I wanted to hear many women tell what had happened to them. Then, even though I had another appointment, I sat down with Elizabeth Rose to learn more about her. My first impression—that she seemed somewhat prone to exaggeration—faded as her story unfolded. Her achievements had indeed been dramatic.

"Not much was known about my illness, or chemical poisoning, when I went down," she said. "So I spent three years trying experimental treatments. After I'd made some progress physically I worked to heal myself emotionally. It's a miracle I'm alive."

To help others get well, she kept a diary that was later published as a book, *Lady of Gray: Healing Candida.* She created and recorded audio cassettes on healing. And in addition to counseling sick individuals, she is a vocal environmental activist working to reduce the ever-increasing causes of environmental illness.

◆ ◆ ◆

Several months later I flew back to Los Angeles to interview Elizabeth Rose in her home, a white town house shaded by palms, where she lives with two daughters. She maintains an office at home for her many projects.

Like Joni and Donna, Elizabeth Rose made use of self-empowerment more than once. The first time was when she extricated herself from an abusive, dysfunctional family; the second time, when she realized she had to divorce; and a third time, when she struggled to save herself from a severe illness. In this chapter we will focus on her recovery, as she completes the process and takes up a survivor mission.

Elizabeth Rose grew up in New York City in an Irish-Italian neighborhood between Ninth and Eleventh Avenues known as Hell's Kitchen. Most buildings in the area were five-story brick tenements with front stoops. Her family lived on the fifth floor in what was called a railroad flat. Like their neighbors, Elizabeth Rose's family didn't own a car or a television set and used scrub boards to wash their clothes.

When she was only four years old, she had an experience that still haunts her. Her six-year-old sister had taken her to the movies in their Times Square neighborhood. After the movie, as the two young girls walked out of the theater, a man approached Elizabeth Rose and asked if she'd like to pick flowers in Central Park. She thought he looked like a priest in her parish and told her sister she was going with him.

He held her hand as they walked along Ninth Avenue toward Fifty-seventh Street. He told her about his daughter, who was eleven years old and who visited him all the time.

♦ ♦ ♦

"We take her clothes off," he said, "and I put my fingers down there and play with her and she plays with my ding-a-ling." "My daddy doesn't do that," Elizabeth Rose said. "All fathers do that," he said.

When they got to Central Park he took her into the bushes and pulled her pants down. On his knees, he took something out of his pants, which to Elizabeth Rose looked like a policeman's night stick. He held her down and tried to put it in her, but she pushed him away and started to run.

"When I got home I was still crying about the awful man. My father put me on the couch and pulled my pants down to look. 'Did he do something? Did something get done to you?' he said. He must have seen bruises near my vagina because he shouted, 'You goddamned filthy slut. You seduced him, you little whore.'

"My mother stood there and did nothing. I thought I must have done something dreadful because my mother ignored me and my father was mad at me."

"My father was a good-looking, dark-haired Irishman who was a route driver at night for a New York daily newspaper. He'd grown up in Hell's Kitchen in a family of thirteen kids. His father was an abusive alcoholic and my father had learned to be tough just to survive. He drank a lot and became an alcoholic, too.

"After my sisters and I were born, he started to beat my mother. My mother was blonde, warm, and loving. When my father married her, he described her in a poem as an innocent flower.

"Even though my mother was faithful, he was insanely

♦ ♦ ♦

suspicious and jealous. He put a piece of cardboard in the lock of their apartment door so when he came in at night, if no one had been there, the cardboard would fall. If it didn't, he was sure my mother was seeing other men.

"One time, when the cardboard didn't fall, he ripped the entire door out of its frame, crawled under the bed, and tipped it over. He was looking for men. He said there were at least ten she was doing it with. We heard him punching her, like she was a punching bag. Then we heard them doing it.

"He was so worried about other men, he wouldn't allow my mother out of the house. We had to go to the grocery store for her. When the priest came to visit, she told him that she wanted to leave my father. But the priest said that her husband was her cross to bear.

"One night we woke up and heard my mother crying. We went into the kitchen. My mother was on her knees and my father had a knife at her throat. He said she was having sex with other men and he was going to kill her.

"We screamed, 'Daddy, don't kill Mommy.'

"He stopped and put the knife down. Then he said, 'You'll find out what a whore your mother is when you grow up.' We had no idea what a whore was.

"Before I started school, at about four, I used the same language I heard at home to the nuns passing by. When they heard me say words like cocksucker, prick and fuck, they told my father. He took a bar of soap, put it into my mouth, and said that he didn't want to hear any more goddamned fucking language like that out of my mouth ever again.

"At home I shut down and became withdrawn. But in school I was outgoing. I was at the top of my class and the nuns

◆ ◆ ◆

praised me. I don't ever remember learning how to read. I always knew.

"When I was eight my mother had twin boys. Because they were red-haired, my father said they weren't his and refused to touch them. I remember her cradling one in each arm. I wanted so badly to be held like that, but she said I was too big.

"I was tall and heavy and a tough kid on the streets, always in fights with boys. When my father wanted to show me how to box, I told him girls didn't box. He beat me up, then made me learn.

"By the time I was nine, I was the only one in the family who could handle him. Whenever he came in drunk, my mother got me out of bed. Frozen with fear, I had to stand there and say, 'Nice, Daddy.' 'Eat the food, Daddy.' 'Put the knife down, Daddy.'

"The next year I fell through a cellar door, twisted like a pretzel, and landed on my back. That night I woke up in terrible pain, but my father called me a phoney. I had a crushed disc that wasn't treated until I was in my thirties."

When Elizabeth Rose was fourteen, her mother tried to kill herself. She climbed up on the windowsill and stepped out on the ledge. Elizabeth Rose grabbed her housedress, pulled her back in, and comforted her. She found a doctor and signed her mother into a psychiatric hospital.

"My mother came back a zombie. She couldn't remember who she was and talked in a monotone. She started drinking every night. With my mother in that condition, it felt to me like she had died. And as far as I was concerned, because of

◆ ◆ ◆

my father's behavior, it felt to me like he had died when I was nine. After that, I felt I had no parents."

To make up for what she missed in her own family, Elizabeth Rose gravitated toward people she could learn from. She seemed to sense instinctively the importance of others' examples, even sought them out.

"I went to the New York Public Library, around the corner, and took out books on women I admired. I read the nurse series about pretty girls who married doctors. It was all sweet and wonderful. I read about the woman who started social work in the United States. The Clara Barton series was my favorite.

"And there were women in the neighborhood who showed me there were other ways to live. One had her own business, a butcher shop that sold meat to all the top New York restaurants. Her sister worked with her and I hung around the shop and watched them work. They taught me how to bake, and I could talk to them about what was going on in our flat. My mother didn't want anybody to know about the beatings or my father's drinking. She said he wasn't an alcoholic because he only drank five nights a week. But the women in the butcher shop let me talk about what was really happening.

"Another woman in the neighborhood was the only college educated woman I knew. She noticed how I talked—I said 'foist' for first—and she taught me to speak correctly.

"The most important person was my aunt, who was also my godmother. She was my father's sister, the last of the thirteen children. She was strong, beautiful, and loving. She was marvelous to me. She always brought me gifts. My birthdays were important to her. Best of all, I was important to her. She took me out and spent time with me. She listened to me. She was my real fairy godmother.

"Her husband, my uncle, adored her. I looked at my mother, who was getting beat up all the time, and at my aunt, who had a loving man. My uncle couldn't do enough for her. He wasn't someone you could walk on, either, and I respected him. I decided he was the type of husband I wanted. I didn't want a macho man, a wife beater, an alcoholic, or a jealous man. I wanted a man like my uncle.

"I watched my godmother become a career woman. After she had raised her daughter she got a job at the telephone company, became a supervisor, and bought stock in AT&T.

"I decided then that I was going to have a good life and I was going to get out of that nuthouse."

"Senior year of high school, I was seventeen and took all the scholarship tests I could. When I won a New York Regents scholarship to nursing school, I was thrilled. I could live at school and it looked like my door out of the madhouse.

"My mother supported my decision to accept the scholarship, but my father said nurses were whores. I told him I was going anyway."

Elizabeth Rose had longed to leave, but the September day when she was packed and ready to move across town, she felt reluctant to go. She sat with her suitcases on the front stoop, crying. Overweight, she was afraid of meeting new people. She worried that new friends would find out about her crazy family. But then, remembering years of violence and emotional

♦ ♦ ♦

pain, she put her tissues in her pocket, picked up her bags along with her terror, and walked down the steps.

"Nursing school took me into another world. There were girls from Long Island, girls from wealthy families, people who wanted to do something.

"After I got mono and lost twenty-five pounds, suddenly, men were at my feet. They told me I was gorgeous, that I had bedroom eyes. They thought I was a femme fatale, but I wasn't. I did want a boyfriend, but, oh, my God, I was terrified of both men and sex."

After years of watching her father beat her mother, she was so frightened of men that she had to have a drink as soon as she could on her dates. She didn't know then that she was drug sensitive or why only one or two drinks made her drunk. Afraid she might become alcoholic like her father, she drank very little.

"If I went out on a date, I wanted that guy to be the best. And I got the best. No way was I ever going to be treated badly by a man again. I didn't fall in love with any of them. I'd date them for three months, but if they got close to me or said they cared about me, I dumped them. Then I'd sit in my room and cry, feeling terrible pain. I knew I was afraid of men and afraid to love because of my father."

After graduation Elizabeth Rose got a job on the surgical floor of a New York hospital. Until she could afford her own apartment, she lived with her family. Late one afternoon, a strange man, who had been hiding behind the stairwell in the front hall of their building, grabbed her at knifepoint. She wrestled herself free and ran up the five flights to their apartment. She expected her father to be home and hoped he would console her.

♦ ♦ ♦

"You fucking whore!" he yelled. She knew he was drunk. "What did *you* do?"

Almost as tall as he was, she stepped up to her father—the first time she had been physically able to confront him—and clawed his face with her fingernails. "Don't you dare touch me or I'll have you locked up!" she shouted. He backed away, stunned.

The next day she left home and moved into an apartment with a group of nurses.

At the hospital, Elizabeth Rose transferred to the emergency room and met a resident working in surgery. Unaware that he was married, she felt an immediate attraction to him.

"He was Jewish, charismatic, gorgeous, and brilliant. He sat down next to me and he listened to me. He was a guy I could tell anything to and I knew he wouldn't repeat it. He was very sexy. But I knew his type could get anyone he wanted and he wasn't going to get me. I wanted to be the one nobody could get.

"But this doctor turned me on like nobody did. I thought he was going to be the love of my life. When I found out he was married, I didn't want to believe it."

At the same time she learned that her father was terminally ill with bone marrow cancer. She felt ambivalence about losing her father and ambivalence about her growing feelings for the doctor. She thought her father's impending death made her more vulnerable to the doctor's charms, but when he asked her out the first time she refused.

Several months later, he told Elizabeth Rose that his wife

♦ ♦ ♦

had left him. He invited her to dinner at his apartment. As she accepted, she had a vision and thought it might be an omen. "I saw a red flame with a moth and a voice said, 'You are sealing your doom.' But I went anyway. We wound up in bed. This guy was wild; he was terrific; he did everything.

"We became very close and he was like the father I never had. I could let out the hurt child in me and be who I really was with him. I never thought it could be possible to love a man the way I loved him.

"He was my grand passion. I found out later that he wasn't separated, that his wife had gone home to see her family. But it was too late—I was already in love.

"This was my first time loving a man. I knew I was taking a risk to love, but I loved him with everything I had.

"He said he was going to divorce his wife, but then she got pregnant. The night the baby was born I was so upset at him for telling me that he'd decided to stay with his wife that I took an overdose of sleeping pills. There was so much drama. He rushed to my apartment and promised that he'd leave her. I wanted him so much. I thought great sex meant great love."

When her father's condition grew worse, Elizabeth Rose went more often to the hospital to see him. She went alone. After her mental breakdown, her mother wasn't able to do much.

"Without my mother or anyone to help me, I had to make the decision not to hook my father up to any life support systems. I was the last one in the family to see him alive and I had to make the decision to let him die. My childhood wish had finally come true. And I actually got to kill him. But, oh, what that did to me. I felt some relief, but the guilt nearly killed me.

"Then I watched my mother slowly get herself back together. She went out and found a job as a telephone operator in a hotel. She met the women in the neighborhood and even started dating.

Elizabeth Rose's relationship with the doctor continued to be both passionate and turbulent. Before he left for army duty at Fort Bragg, he separated from his wife and asked Elizabeth Rose to give up her job and follow him. But soon after she arrived he complained that she weighed too much and announced that he was going back to his wife. Elizabeth Rose was heartbroken, returned to New York, and moved in with her mother.

Despondent, she stopped eating. "I wanted to die. I was really in despair. I wasn't trying to control anything or anybody by not eating. I wanted to die, that's all."

The doctor tried to reach her often by phone, but she refused all his calls. Later, when she did talk to him, he convinced her to return to his base. He had divorced and their reunion was bittersweet. When he asked her to marry him, she heard an inner voice warning her not to. Despite her misgivings, they were married several days later.

"I had been drawn to him because he made me feel intelligent, beautiful, and like the sexiest woman he had ever known. But after we were married he criticized my looks,

♦ ♦ ♦

my speech, my weight. And I rarely saw him. I guess he thought once he had me he didn't have to pay attention to me anymore.

"As soon as I was pregnant, he started seeing other women. He flaunted these relationships. He even kissed my girlfriend in front of me.

"I tried to cover up my pain by drinking and not telling anyone. People came up to me and said he was so attractive and charming and I was lucky to be married to him. I would agree and thank them, but inside I was suffering tremendously. Who would believe Mr. Wonderful was so sick? I felt alone and trapped.

"When our first daughter was born, I had strange reactions to the anaesthesia and pain medication—like seeing leaves and grass coming to life—while I was at the hospital. I still didn't know that I was allergic to most drugs. When I got home my husband was so ashamed of my behavior he got angry and told me to go back to my mother.

"While our daughter was still an infant, he started bringing other men and women home for sex. I was horrified. He'd never done anything like that before. But I still loved him and had to drink to cope with my rage and the realization that he didn't love me.

"The following year our second daughter was born. With two babies to care for, I felt overwhelmed and noticed I was becoming impatient with the older daughter. I started to abuse her verbally, not physically. Well, I did smack her around a bit.

"I saw myself becoming just like both my parents—cruel, like my father, and not strong enough to get out, like my

♦ ♦ ♦

mother. I was devastated at what I'd become—everything I had worked all my life not to be."

The family moved to the West Coast and built an enormous one-story glass house on a cliff overlooking the Pacific Ocean. "I was thirty, had a beautiful home, and drove a Mercedes. According to the American Dream, I had made it. But those things didn't matter to me—I was in such emotional and physical pain.

"Taking care of the children aggravated my old back injury from the fall through the cellar door. Even though I could hardly move, my husband told me to get out of bed and take care of the children.

"I felt like I was living a *Gaslight* existence. I was Ingrid Bergman and he was Charles Boyer plotting to drive me out of my mind.

"Our second child was born with multiple birth defects and cried every night with colic. Even though I was strong, I didn't feel I could cope anymore and asked to be signed into a hospital, one of the places Marilyn Monroe had been to. A psychiatrist there was the first support I felt I had. He told me that with therapy I'd be okay, that I did not have to feel my life was doomed because I had chosen a man as sick as my father.

"While I was there I decided to go to work again, to take care of myself, and to become independent of him. I made a plan to be sure the kids were taken care of and to have a career where I could make money."

After she left the hospital even though Elizabeth Rose felt

♦ ♦ ♦

strong enough to bring up the subject of divorce with her husband, she planned instead to finish school first.

Before she could start school, her old back injury caused problems and she made an appointment for surgery. She dreaded the needed surgery because she was certain to have almost psychotic reactions to the medications she would be given. Despite her fear, she went ahead and endured the hallucinations and agony caused by the drugs.

While she recuperated, she applied to colleges. With a three-year nursing degree, she needed only one more year of college to earn her B.A. From there she wanted to go to law school.

"Even though I had to wear a huge back brace to college, classes were wonderful. I was back in my youth because school was where I'd been praised. The professors loved me and I was at the top of my class. I was in my element again."

Elizabeth Rose graduated magna cum laude and was accepted at law school. Excited about these accomplishments, she regained some of her earlier optimism.

"Just as I felt ready to divorce, a strange health problem appeared. I first noticed it while biking along the beach. Suddenly one day, I just couldn't breathe. It felt like there was cement in my lungs. I was in terrible pain but thought it was caused by the smog that day. My doctor put me in the hospital and found a blood clot in my lung.

"It happened again a few months later, when I took the girls on a vacation to Hawaii. I got off the plane, gasping for air, and turned gray. The doctor who examined me couldn't find anything wrong.

◆ ◆ ◆

"Several days later, the pains in my chest were so bad I was put into the intensive care unit. They found more than one hundred black spots on my lungs. I was terrified, and I couldn't find out what was happening to me.

"The pain in my chest was unbearable. I felt like I was being crushed, and I had to let them give me a shot of pain medication. The next thing I knew I was on the ceiling looking down on my very gray body in the hospital bed. Doctors and nurses were hovering around; tubes and equipment were everywhere. Then my picture went blank.

"The next morning I asked the nurse what had happened. 'After we gave you the shot for pain last night,' she said, 'you almost died.' "

Back home in California, she went from doctor to doctor looking for an explanation for her chest pains and the spots in her lungs. As she continued to deteriorate, a second emergency operation was needed on her back.

"In the middle of these devastating health problems, divorce proceedings began. My husband tried to pull me down. He dragged me through the courts, attempting to destroy me. He subpoened doctors to say I was a phony, although some ended up testifying against him. He knew how much I loved our girls and wanted to raise them, so he threatened to take them from me. He made up lies and all kinds of charges to avoid alimony or child support. One of the things a man like that can't take is parting with his money."

While she battled for a fair settlement for herself and her children, she never anticipated its devastating result. When the issues of the divorce were finally resolved, Elizabeth Rose

♦ ♦ ♦

was awarded nearly everything she had asked for. "I won, but if you consider the cost mentally, emotionally, and physically, I lost. And the love of my life was gone. The minute the divorce was final, he married the latest girlfriend. I didn't think I could survive it."

After the divorce Elizabeth Rose had intended to begin law school, but her health problems prevented it. She often slipped into life-threatening shock in new buildings, the beauty shop, and the grocery store. Three times she passed out in restaurants and paramedics were called in to revive her. Exhausted all the time, she was frustrated not knowing what was wrong.

"I had paranoia, hallucinations, fear, anxiety, and depression. I started to crave ice cream and peanuts. If I didn't eat one or the other I began to sweat, feel faint, and my blood pressure dropped. Only huge amounts, like a half gallon of ice cream or a pound of peanuts, helped. But after eating all that, my hands and feet turned blue, I got confused, and I began to lose consciousness. Forcing myself to vomit stopped the symptoms.

"I had this whole secret life going on and felt so ashamed. I tried but still couldn't find anyone to tell me what was wrong."

She finally found a doctor who discovered she was allergic to most foods, including milk products, grains, nuts, and fruits. She was also allergic to the chemicals found in shampoo, soap, detergents, cosmetics, carpets, paint, furniture, mattresses, synthetic clothing, wallboards, floors, cars, and gas heating.

Hoping he was wrong, Elizabeth Rose consulted an immunologist. But he confirmed the diagnosis and explained that her immune system had broken down. She could no longer tolerate exposure to most things in the environment. She also had an overgrowth of a normal intestinal fungus, candida. Uncontrolled, the fungus could cause anxiety, fear, paranoia, an excessive appetite for some foods, and fatal toxic reactions.

"He said I had environmental illness (E.I.) with systemic candidiasis. By that he meant I'd become allergic to the twentieth century. His nurse gave me a two-page list of substances to avoid. In other words throw out your house, your car, your children, and yourself, and you'll be all right.

"There had to be a mistake. I stumbled out of the doctor's office, crying hysterically. What had I done to deserve this? Why had this happened to me? I thought I was going to die."

In despair, she drove to the harbor and walked out to the end of the wooden pier. She raved at God. "God, how could you do this to me? I've had major back problems and I'm still in pain with that. I can't take anymore! If you're out there, take away this back pain or this illness." To her surprise, her back pain subsided and she felt a peace descend on her.

She went home and thought. Up to that time she had tried to help herself, but she wasn't convinced that anything she did really mattered. She decided to tell her preadolescent daughters that she might die and asked them if they'd rather live with their father. They wanted to stay with her. Their decision became the impetus to do everything she could to get well.

That night, however, she went into allergic shock. She cried out to her mother, who had died several years ago. "Mom, if you are there, please help me." And she called out to God, "If you are there, please help me."

♦ ♦ ♦

"At that point I accepted the fact that I had E.I. When I stopped fighting it and giving up in despair, my recovery began. My next step was to find out what I could do. From then on, I believed I could be healed completely. All I had to learn was how."

To Elizabeth Rose, accepting a grave illness on top of what she thought of as a lifetime of abuse seemed almost impossible.

She knew that her problems growing up had led to problems in her marriage and with her health. And as an abused child and wife, Elizabeth Rose was not only used to trauma, but she had practiced what Ellen Bass and Laura Davis refer to in their book, *The Courage to Heal,* as "the basics" of coping. Elizabeth Rose was accustomed to minimizing, rationalizing, denying, and forgetting. "Minimizing," Bass and Davis write, "means pretending that whatever happened wasn't really that bad. . . . Rationalizing is the means by which children explain away abuse. . . . Denying is turning your head the other way and pretending that whatever is happening isn't, or what has happened didn't. . . . Forgetting is one of the most common and effective ways. . . . The human mind has tremendous powers of repression."

With the defenses Elizabeth Rose had built up and used over and over, first with her father, then with her husband, and finally with her illness, it was a wonder she could break through them to come to acceptance. She was deeply disturbed by all that had happened to her; feelings of abandonment had led to assessing herself as "bad and defective." "The child becomes an object of contempt to herself," John Bradshaw writes in *Lears*. "And because she is contemptible, she can no longer be herself; she must give up her authentic being and become a false self. This loss of her I-am-ness is a deep spiritual wound that sets up a chronic low-grade depression—a kind of frozen, unresolved grief."

Elizabeth Rose's unresolved grief was destroying her health. Before she could get well, she would have to find a way to heal herself of all past abuse. Breaking through such powerful defenses to begin that process was an act of courage and faith.

One of her first steps was to find a therapist. "Zena was wonderful. That lady listened to me. Neither of us knew how difficult the next few years would be. I was too ill to leave home, so we worked together by phone." Elizabeth Rose's next step was to look for help for her illness, even though there were no known treatments and environmental illness could be fatal. She heard about a support group of E.I. sufferers in San Francisco. She called a few of them. Most were too ill to help but she found Eve, who was also fighting for her life. While talking to Eve, Elizabeth Rose felt encouraged.

"Eve's loving voice on the phone did more for my state than any drug could have. When you are unable to love yourself, let others love you. We do need people. We must learn to take what they can offer."

With Eve's guidance, Elizabeth Rose set to work to recover physically. She began by adapting her life-style to her allergies. After hiring a nurse's aide to care for her and her girls, she stayed in the house alone in her bedroom. Each day she put on the same cotton jeans and cotton blouse—the only clothes that didn't cause a reaction. She couldn't bathe with soap, use deodorant, or wash her hair with shampoo. She could drink only distilled water and eat just six kinds of vegetables.

"During the first month, confined to my room, I lost thirty pounds. While still experimenting to find out what I could tolerate, and close to death, I often had hallucinations. My skin turned gray, red, purple, blue, and yellow. My brain swelled. I blacked out. I vomited. My entire childhood came back to me and poured out, just poured out."

Because Elizabeth Rose was drug sensitive, using drugs for treatment put her at risk. She began by trying nystatin, a drug that could cause her physical and psychological reactions. She wrote in her journal to keep track of its effects.

"The tenth day of nystatin brought misery. My face turned red and burning. Numbness enveloped my hands, and cerebrals surfaced again—fear, paranoia, insanity, and depression. . . . I increased the dosage a tiny bit. Everything started to go black. Faint. Legs leaden."

But after three weeks on the drug she thought she felt well enough to go into her living room, where there were newspapers and magazines. In the past she had reacted to printer's ink. But this time she didn't. When she returned to her room she wrote, "No longer did I see one paragraph faded, the next jet black; no longer did I smell all chemicals in every product one hundred times normal. I was healing!"

In addition to the medication prescribed by her doctor, she tried other treatments. She drank a tea made from tree bark.

◆ ◆ ◆

"After a few sips, I felt weak. Once again faintness and dizziness gripped me. Too much for my body right now along with nystatin."

Two weeks later when she tried the tea again, she felt a flow of energy. She called Eve with her joy.

Elizabeth Rose felt intuitively that staying alive would require emotional healing as well. "With Zena's help, I worked on mourning the tragedies in my life that had led in part to making me so sick—a lack of love as a child, including deep rage and anger at the abuse I'd suffered.

"During acute symptoms of physical cleansing a simultaneous emotional regurgitation occurs. Every negative incident in your life reappears in no specific order. . . . I found myself reexperiencing events I thought I'd put behind me, resolved. Every event we've ever lived is stored somewhere in the body. . . . Therefore as your body heals, so do the emotions.

"I had believed that my parents had abandoned me emotionally when the truth was they didn't know what to do. My belief was a destructive one, destroying my self-esteem. When I let go of a false idea, some form of healing always followed."

Elizabeth Rose was no stranger to networking, having discovered its benefits at an early age. An abused and lonely child longing for someone to look up to, she had found role models in her neighborhood and in books. Near the end of her marriage, believing that she was going crazy, she had found reassurance from a male psychiatrist and her friends.

As she took on the challenge of her illness, Zena and Eve

♦ ♦ ♦

became the two critical figures supporting Elizabeth Rose in her recovery. She worked with Zena to heal emotionally and with Eve, an empowering example, to heal physically.

Talking to these women each step of the way gave her allies and diminished her feelings of helplessness. With Zena listening, she could face and release past pain; with Eve advising, she tried unusual treatments. Both women nurtured and affirmed Elizabeth Rose, helping her to build self-value, especially challenging for someone so accustomed to thinking that she was flawed, that something was wrong with her, that she was bad.

Not fully aware of what she was doing, Elizabeth Rose was using support to heal the wounded child within. Following healing stages similar to those outlined by Friel and Friel in *An Adult Child's Guide to What Is "Normal,"* Elizabeth Rose was identifying the wrongs that happened to her as a child; she was having her feelings about them; she was embracing those feelings; and she was not just talking about them but she was also sharing them.

Even before she was fully recovered Elizabeth Rose was invited to speak to a Cancer Control Group, an organization interested in ways of healing from degenerative diseases. When she reminded them that she didn't have cancer, they said they wanted to hear her story because she was recovering from an illness that could be fatal. She was also invited to speak to the local H.E.A.L. chapter about what she was doing to recover.

She was not only well enough to give talks, she was also well enough to enjoy her growing daughters. She took them to the movies and played games with them. Always alert to what she was learning about recovery, she returned home after a day with her daughters and wrote a note to herself, "Revert to childish pleasures to get through this."

After reading an article about Pope John Paul II's ability to forgive his would-be assassin, Elizabeth Rose felt motivated to add a spiritual dimension to her healing process. "Forgiveness brings freedom to the person forgiving. In my desperate hours I prayed to learn to forgive more thoroughly in order that I might be completely healed.

"Through letting go of resentments and bitterness toward any person, place, or thing, the body heals. Through forgiveness, I found self-love.

"Before I got critically ill, I believed totally in self-reliance and super-independence. . . . I verbally crucified anyone who believed in God. Weaklings. Need to believe some invisible source is helping them. Good for the masses. Gives them hope. Not for me; I'm too self-sufficient.

"Getting sick, I was forced to reach inside myself for something more powerful than myself. Never would I have been humbled sufficiently without being fatally ill. After yelling in pain for help from God and feeling a flood of warmth flow through my body and the pain or shock go away, I told myself there must be something to this.

"Eventually I found out that self-reliance had limits, while reliance on a Higher Power brought limitless possibilities. I learned to depend on a power outside myself. That's true power."

Whenever she felt frustrated, in pain, or tempted to give up, she used prayer. Then she added meditation, visualization, imaging, and laughter to keep herself going.

♦ ♦ ♦

"Daily prayer of any kind heals. I use the Twenty-third Psalm and the Saint Francis of Assisi prayer.

"Meditation in any orthodox form is difficult in acute phases of this illness. All I could do was take a deep breath and count as far as I could. Then I blew out every ounce of air, mentally releasing anger, rage, depression, bitterness, self-pity, or fear. A great deal of repair of the cells plus serenity began from this humble exercise. Later I was able to meditate daily, fifteen to twenty minutes in the morning and before bed. My healing progressed as my ability to meditate increased.

"Visualizing a peaceful place, a place I wanted to be, like the beach or mountains, helped me to heal.

"Imaging is a powerful form of self-hypnosis. I envisioned specific body parts and surrounded them with white or pink light. I also pretended that my nervous system was a tree of life. I sent pink light to all its branches and repeated to myself 'I am well.'

"Humor is another way to tap inner resources. Laughter pulled me through many emotionally devastating moments. . . .

By choosing both traditional and alternative ways of healing, one after another and on several levels, Elizabeth Rose herself was changing. A personality change—learning to forgive others, to let go of the past, and to value herself—was necessary for Elizabeth Rose to recover. In *Love, Medicine and Miracles,* Bernie Siegel comments that personality change is hard, but there are two ways to make it easier. First, by working with a supportive therapy group or sharing honestly with trusted loved ones; second, by regular meditation in which you visualize yourself as you want to become.

Out of her intention to get well Elizabeth Rose made choices that determined the difference between a life that worked and a life that didn't work. With support, she had learned to see her chances to choose. She considered what methods and activities could be useful to her and pursued those that produced results.

"Today I am convinced that if I were to reproduce the events that led to my breakdown—ignoring physical limits, overachieving, returning to a toxic diet, alcohol, toxic thinking, and severe stress—I could resurrect the entire disease. The lesson for me was to change to a conscious loving attitude toward myself, on a daily basis.

"One isn't greeted with much sympathy with this condition. There are several reactions by fellow humans—fear, avoidance, all-in-your-head clichés, and abandonment. Most people with E.I. are abandoned by spouses, lovers, friends, and families. Therefore it is essential not to abandon yourself. Self-love is a must.

"Disease is an opportunity to learn to love yourself."

After accepting her illness, working on healing through networking and choosing, Elizabeth Rose had learned to love herself. With self-love, shifting to another level of commitment naturally followed.

By giving herself 100 percent to her recovery, she reached a point where she saw "limitless possibilities" for herself.

♦ ♦ ♦

When she had been trapped in her condition, she saw no possibilities, only limits. At that time the prospect of such a restricted future made her wish for no future at all.

As a result of healing through self-empowerment, she moved way past physical recovery until she felt at peace with past abuse. She had become capable of reaching out to others who were still suffering and wanted to give away what had been given to her.

At the end of our last session together, while talking in the living room of her town house, she said, "After those three years, I was healed of a great deal of lifelong abuse. Many gifts came to me, including the gift of healing.

"I began spending time with fellow sufferers. One woman, a former nun, came to me—gray, with almost no pulse. She'd been exposed to formaldehyde and was in shock. I playe her one of the tapes I'd made to help people heal—from the inside out.

"I placed my hands on her, and all this energy flowed through me and I saw her turn pink, her pulse went to normal, and her pain disappeared. When I asked her what happened, she said that halfway through the tape something flooded her being. I hugged her and said, 'There is a God and he loves you.'

"The more I helped others, the more power emanated through me. When I was healing myself, I had to learn to love myself. Now I was helping other people to love themselves.

"I've gone through intense emotional suffering, transcending my limits. None of this has been easy, and I don't want

♦ ♦ ♦

it to come across as such. I've been on the floor feeling as if my guts would come out, but making decisions to grow. I'm no superwoman. I've been through the same feelings that everyone goes through.

"I went through the pain of walking through the feelings that were crippling me, but I still did it. I consciously clung to a higher power to survive and it worked. Some part of me knew that there was no other way to go. I knew all good things had to come from that. That was the direction. It felt right."

From shifting, Elizabeth Rose had moved almost immediately to mentoring. She felt a need to work with and for other people. Even before she was well, she had given talks on recovering.

"Now I'm working on problems of the environment. I give lectures, I'm a guest on radio and television shows. I've made tapes on how to heal from E.I. and I personally counsel very ill people. I'm an activist, alerting the public to potentially toxic chemicals. I hope to stop the spread of this deadly illness."

With the same energy that went into getting herself well, she committed herself to helping other people get well. She started spiritual recovery groups. She seemed to know as she wrote in her diary each day that her words would some day serve other victims of disease.

In the preface to her book, *Lady of Gray: Healing Candida,* she wrote, "Without the need to help allay your suffering through sharing my experience . . . this book would not have been written. . . ."

Other survivors have also used writing about their expe-

♦ ♦ ♦

riences as a way of helping themselves and others. Robert Jay Lifton, in *Death in Life: Survivors of Hiroshima,* describes a Japanese woman who became one of the best known writers of A-bomb literature. She was "carried from her house unconscious by her mother and sister . . . she began to write as a form of survivor mission and a means of staying alive."

William Styron's mission in writing *Darkness Visible: A Memoir of Madness* was quoted in the *New York Times Book Review.* "I was chagrined to discover how many people had a total misapprehension of what this illness is. My need to communicate overrode the risks of self-exposure. The rewards have been immense. I was able to be the voice for a lot of people."

Being a voice for many is one characteristic found among those who change themselves, triumph over adversity, and reach mentoring. Other characteristics, as observed by psychologist Al Siebert of Portland, Oregon, are that survivors:

—have empathy for other people, even opponents;
—use subliminal perception or intuition as a valid, useful source of information;
—have good timing, especially when speaking or taking an original action;
—recognize early clues about possible developments and take meaningful action;
—rapidly assimilate new or unexpected experiences and facilitate being changed by them;
—feel comfortable in complex, ambiguous situations that might bewilder others;
—keep a positive direction and show self-confidence against sustained, adverse circumstances;

• • •

—rely successfully on inner resources in disruptive situations;
—have a talent for serendipity and are able to convert accidents or misfortunes into something useful.

By converting accidents or misfortunes into something useful for themselves and others, all of the women in this book made their lives extraordinary. Donna, a television anchorwoman in a wheelchair, provides a highly visible example of what's possible to those with disabilities. Lauren's reversal of a destitute life of heroin and prostitution resulted in advocacy work for women. Out of Kim's homelessness she uncovered her talents as a leader and used them to help other homeless mothers get off welfare. Patty's successful fight with drugs shaped a career with other troubled teens. Stephanie's debilitating divorce made her strong enough to show other divorced women how to put their lives back on track. After Joni's disabling ski accident, she became a triathlete capable of motivating other people to go for their personal best. Marie's triumph over addiction enabled her to guide fourteen hundred addicted women to health. And Elizabeth Rose's long battle with illness led her to become a lecturer, environmental activist, and author.

Elizabeth Rose expressed her feelings about this final stage of self-empowerment, as many of the others have. "I had to go through all of this to become who I am, and to do the work I'm doing. I was given these gifts through suffering. I can keep them only through service."

Making Your Own Life Extraordinary

♦ ♦ ♦

10 USING THE SELF-EMPOWERMENT PROCESS

Each woman in this book told her intimate story for two reasons. First, for herself, because sharing in this way is integral to her "survivor mission." And second, for you, because she believes her transformation can be a catalyst for you to claim longed-for changes in your life.

All of them want to serve as your empowering examples.

◆ ◆ ◆

They hope that their revelations will motivate you to move in new directions: to hold a mirror up to yourself, to evaluate disturbing situations, and to begin turning your dreams into reality, as they did.

And now it is your turn to make your life extraordinary. Perhaps you feel that the problems in your life aren't nearly as formidable or urgent as those you've just read about. For example, you may not have a life-threatening illness to monitor daily as Elizabeth Rose does, but you'd be happier if you had more energy. Or the man in your life doesn't abuse you the way the men in Lauren's life did, you just wish he could be more sensitive to your needs. Because your problems aren't as dire as those described here, you can feel optimistic about the benefits of using self-empowerment. But if you are coping with a severe problem such as illness, a disability, an addiction, or a loss, you can feel encouraged by these women—hearing what a difference the principles of self-empowerment can make.

Thus, I can't think of any reason for you not to begin using this process to make your own life extraordinary. Remembering that Patty began at nine, you know you can't be too young to start. And, of course, you know that it's never too late when you look at the changes Marie made while in her fifties. So now, with no excuses or rationalizations, this is the time for you to empower yourself to make a change.

Most of you already know which problem you want to begin to work on. But for those of you who want help clarifying which area needs your attention first, you can try a meditative exercise. While sitting quietly alone or taking a walk by yourself, consider these questions:

What have I been putting up with? What do I wish I could do something about?

♦ ♦ ♦

What do I plan to handle someday, but don't think I can right now?

What is preventing me from having my life be all that it can be?

When you've determined which challenge you are going to take on, begin by accepting the problem as realistically as possible. You'll recall that there's a critical difference between acknowledging a problem and accepting it. When you can accept your problem, you'll sense it on a deep emotional level, you'll feel it's impact, and you'll tell the truth about it.

After articulating and taking responsibility for a specific project, you'll want to find support—solid, unconditional support—through networking. Consider what resources you already have. And to make new connections with other people who can encourage you, ask yourself these questions:

Do I know anyone who has accomplished what I now want to do?

Do I have a friend or family member who is sympathetic to my cause?

Have I read a profile about someone who has done what I want to do? Could I write to that person and ask for recommendations for support people?

Is there a member of the clergy, doctor, or therapist I could ask for suggestions?

Can I attend meetings of such support groups as Alcoholics Anonymous, Al-Anon, Ala-teen, Overeaters Anonymous, Narcotics Anonymous, or Gamblers Anonymous to talk with someone about the concept of support?

Once you've found support to help you make the change you want, you've taken a major step forward. You are moving away from wishing or hoping for change toward real possibility.

A requisite part of this process that can take you from possibility to dreams-come-true is considering how you view yourself, how you feel about yourself. Like Donna, you may have come from a family where you were nurtured, valued, and affirmed, giving you a head start on making necessary changes and the confidence to meet a crisis head-on. Or, as many of the women in this book did, you may feel a need to improve your self-value. You may want to begin your work with support people by requesting their help to raise your level of self-confidence and self-respect. Those who've had debilitating early relationships or have a genetic tendancy toward low self-value need strong backing and encouragement to gradually believe in and care about themselves. They can take heart, however, from several of the women here. Many of them suffered as children but through self-empowerment they recreated themselves and their lives.

Support is essential not only at the beginning of your project but all the way along. As you head toward an objective—which could be anything from recovering from an eating disorder to getting physically fit—ask your support people for guidance whenever you need it. Each time you get to a crossroads, talk it over with someone before you act, as Patty did when her boyfriend got married and she wanted to drink. If you get discouraged, feel low, need a boost, call one of the people who supports you before you give in or give up. To the degree that you respond to others' interest, encouragement, and love, you will be able to stay on course.

As you notice an improvement in yourself and see wonderful changes taking place, continue to stay close to the people

♦ ♦ ♦

supporting you. Enjoy their praise for choosing wisely. Their enthusiastic feedback is part of this process. Let it lead you to the next, and then the next, positive decision or action. Eventually you'll get accustomed to doing what's best for yourself and won't need to check in as often. You'll sense your own improving ability not only to recognize but also to take those ever-present chances to choose.

After making a series of beneficial decisions, as Joni did following her skiing accident and again as she took up running, you'll experience a difference in your attitude and approach. You'll be living the change you've been working toward: you'll have initiated a positive shift. You'll like the ways a shift feels. With shifting comes commitment, freedom, serenity, often joy.

As you accumulate accomplishments and feel good about your change, begin mentoring. Look for someone you can guide. When you become a role model, able to motivate other people to help themselves, you become a link in this powerful people chain. Just as Kim did when she helped other homeless women find jobs and places to live, you will reinforce your own commitment to independence and self-reliance. When you are asked to help another person reach her goals, as Stephanie was asked by other divorced women, you'll say yes. And each time you begin with a beginner, as Marie did with addicts, you'll be reminded of where you once were and how much you prefer where you are now.

It isn't a coincidence that the women in *Ordinary Women, Extraordinary Lives* devote part or all of their time to helping others. Patty, Lauren, Joni, Marie, and Elizabeth Rose have careers in which other people benefit from their experience and expertise. Donna, Stephanie, and Kim have professions or jobs in addition to service to others. As a result of their

• • •

personal victories, being a role model comes naturally to all of them. They don't consider themselves do-gooders; their work fulfills and sustains them. And it will strengthen you.

Finding and Giving Support

In addition to working with the individuals supporting you, you'll benefit by being part of a group. There are many support groups set up for a wide range of purposes such as bereavement and death, health and disabilities, mental health, parenting and family, as well as Twelve-Step Recovery groups. If you can't find a local self-help group to give you the support you need as you go through self-empowerment, consider starting one.

If you decide to begin a group, look for others who would like encouragement as they initiate or complete work on their individual projects. One effective way to form a group is by word of mouth. Talk about your intentions to your friends and colleagues who in turn will tell their friends. If you need to reach out into your community to find a group of six to twelve women, run a small ad in your local paper, distribute flyers, or post an announcement—at the post office, grocery store, drug store, or bank—inviting others to assist you in starting a support group.

You might call your new group an Extraordinary Lives Support Group. For the location of your first meeting, select a common space at a library or community center. Churches, synagogues, and hospitals sometimes make meeting rooms available.

At your first meeting, discuss the purpose of the group. A

♦ ♦ ♦

sample "purpose" or "mission statement," to use as a source for that discussion, might be the following:

—to help each other use self-empowerment to accomplish our objectives;
—to learn to view our problems as projects;
—to support the changes we see in each other; and
—to continue to empower others to grow and change.

At your initial meeting, allow a few minutes for each participant to introduce herself and talk about her interests and challenges, particularly the specific project she wants support for. Talk about guidelines appropriate for your group and share phone numbers for on-going support between meetings. Ask someone to "chair" the next meeting; then determine the time, place, and location of future meetings.

As group members make progress and reach their objectives, it's important to keep your group going. Newcomers need to hear and see the women who've been successful and benefitted from the group's support, just as models need newcomers to give them an opportunity to reinforce their changes.

If you begin an E.L. group or if your group has a success story to report, I'd be happy to hear from you. Write to me in care of the publisher. And any time, whether or not you are in a group, that you begin self-empowerment, I'd be interested in what you plan to work on and who will be supporting you.

When you reach the final stage of self-empowerment I'd like to know how your triumph, change, or success translates into service—your own "survivor mission." As Gail Sheehy

♦ ♦ ♦

writes in "The Victorious Personality" in *The New York Times Magazine,* "One may be born with a naturally resilient temperament, but one develops a victorious personality. Those who do often come to believe they are special, perhaps meant to serve a purpose beyond themselves."

A Final Note of Encouragement to the Reader

♦ ♦ ♦

Quite unexpectedly, writing this book became a journey through self-empowerment. I had a dream—to celebrate several remarkable women through the vehicle of their own stories while communicating to you how they had gone from victim to victor. At first my intention seemed simple enough. And before I began I had no idea how hard that would be or how much persistence it would take or that I would depend on the five stages of the very process I was writing about to do it.

◆ ◆ ◆

Early in the project I sat at my word processor with transcripts of the taped interviews trying out a variety of formats and styles. I soon saw the need for accepting that the book I had wanted to write for so long was going to be far more challenging than I had anticipated. But I felt that if I gave up, the women to be profiled would be disappointed and I didn't want to let them down. As important, I felt certain their common message would matter to thousands of other people.

I was still experimenting and struggling with how this book might work when I started networking. A group of writers, we'd met in a writing course at Radcliffe College, decided to meet regularly to give each other feedback on our current pursuits. Every two weeks, each month, for the past several years, we have sat around an oval dining room table in Cambridge, Massachusetts, talking about our work.

Encouragement from Barbara, Elizabeth, and Heidi made all the difference. Their interest in seeing what I had done in the intervening two weeks and the my reluctance to drive two hours each way with no new manuscript pages to show them spurred me on. They didn't hesitate to say, "There should be more of you in there." "Take out some details." "This works better." Soon they were using the new terms, such as empowering example and self-value, naturally in conversations, as if these terms had always been in the language. I was thrilled. They began to talk about using the process themselves and shared their success.

As a result of this support I recognized that I was choosing to continue. I wrote and they read, sometimes the same story, several times, in several forms. If they got tired of it, they never let on.

• • •

I spent eight to ten hours a day writing in my office. One day my husband looked in the door and smiled. "Do you know how many books Stephen King wrote in the past three years? Write faster."

Then, miraculously, the manuscript seemed to take on a life of its own, to have its own energy. The chapters reordered themselves more than once. I just adjusted the table of contents and rearranged the chapters, lined up on my office countertop. The five stages of self-empowerment renamed themselves, and I agreed. One day I began typing an additional chapter about the process, not in my original plan. I went with it, trusting that all this would stop when the pieces came together. And one day they did. Everything seemed to be in place.

This was it! I was happy with the balance between the women's stories and the process. The process was easy to remember, follow, and use. Even though these revelations meant months of rewriting, I was eager to do it. I became aware of shifting, of my commitment to complete the book, of all wavering thoughts being gone. When comments from the group came back, written across various pages—"excellent," "you did it!" and "bravo"—I knew that their support had helped my dream come true.

Mentoring with the group, to me, seemed rather indirect but not to them. One woman said, "I don't know how you did it. I would have given up and gone onto something else long ago. But the way you've stuck with this, you're an example for all of us." That felt good, the long effort surely worthwhile.

Then it struck me as an irony that the very process—designed for you to empower yourself in whatever way you

◆ ◆ ◆

need—had enabled me to write this book. If it hadn't been for self-empowerment, *Ordinary Women, Extraordinary Lives* would not have been written. Emerson was right. "It is one of the most beautiful compensations of this life that no man can seriously help another without helping himself."

Bibliography

♦ ♦ ♦

Anonymous. *Each Day a New Beginning*, Center City, Minnesota: Hazeldon Foundation, 1982.

Baruch, Grace, Rosalind Barnett and Caryl Rivers. *Lifeprints*, New York: McGraw Hill Book Co., 1983.

Bass, Ellen and Laura Davis. *The Courage to Heal*, New York: Harper and Row, 1988.

Bateson, Mary Catherine. *Composing a Life*, New York: The Atlantic Monthly Press, 1989.

Beattie, Melody. *Codependent No More*, New York: Harper and Row, 1987.

Black, Claudia. *Repeat After Me*, Denver Colorado: M.A.C. Printing and Publications, 1985.

Bradshaw, John. "Our Families, Ourselves," *Lears*, March 1989: 95.

◆ ◆ ◆

Flagg, Fannie. "Fear of Prying: A Testimonial to Support Groups," *Lears*, May 1989: 62.

Fitzgerald, Ed. *That Place in Minnesota*, New York: Viking Penguin, 1990.

Friel, John, Ph.D. and Linda Friel, M.A. *An Adult Child's Guide to What's "Normal,"* Deerfield Beach, Florida: Health Communications, Inc., 1990.

Gilligan, Carol. *In a Different Voice*, Cambridge: Harvard University Press, 1982.

Lerner, Harriet, Ph.D. *The Dance of Anger*, New York: Harper and Row, 1985.

Lifton, Robert Jay. *Death in Life: Survivors of Hiroshima*, New York: Random House, 1967.

———. *Home from War*, New York: Simon and Schuster, 1973.

———. *The Broken Connection*, New York: Simon and Schuster, 1979.

Miller, Jean Baker, M.D. *Toward a New Psychology of Women*, Boston: Beacon Press, 1986.

Norwood, Robin. *Women Who Love Too Much*, New York: Pocket Books, 1985.

Peck, M. Scott, M.D. *The Road Less Traveled*, New York: Simon and Schuster, 1978.

Rose, Elizabeth. *Lady of Gray: Healing Candida*, Santa Monica, California: Butterfly Publishing Co., 1985.

Sanford, Linda and Mary Ellen Donovan. *Women and Self-Esteem*, New York: Anchor Press/Doubleday, 1984.

Sheehy, Gail. "The Victorious Personality," *New York Times Magazine*, New York, April 20, 1986.

Siegel, Bernie S., M.D. *Love, Medicine and Miracles*, New York: Harper and Row, 1986.

van der Kolk, Bessel A., M.D. *Psychological Trauma*, Washington, D.C.: American Psychiatric Press, 1987.

Viorst, Judith. *Necessary Losses*, New York: Ballantine Books, 1986.

Wegscheider, Sharon. *Another Chance, Hope and Health for the Alcoholic Family*, Palo Alto, California: Science and Behavior Books, Inc., 1981.

Woititz, Janet. *Struggle for Intimacy*, Deerfield Beach, Florida: Health Communications, Inc., 1985.

Endnotes

♦ ♦ ♦

Chapter One

1. Bernie S. Siegel, M.D., *Love, Medicine and Miracles,* (New York: Harper and Row, 1986), 169.
2. Robert Jay Lifton, *Death in Life: Survivors of Hiroshima,* (New York: Random House, 1967), 304.
3. Jean Baker Miller, M.D., *Toward a New Psychology of Women,* (Boston: Beacon Press, 1986), 31.
4. M. Scott Peck, M.D., *The Road Less Traveled,* (New York: Simon and Schuster, 1978), 16, 30.
5. Melody Beattie, *Codependent No More,* (New York: Harper and Row, 1987), 117.

♦ ♦ ♦

6. Ellen Bass and Laura Davis, *The Courage to Heal,* (New York: Harper and Row, 1988), 174.
7. Judith Lewis Herman, M.D., assistant clinical professor of psychiatry at the Cambridge Hospital, Harvard Medical School, and author of *Father-Daughter Incest*; Nicolina Fedele, Ph.D., assistant clinical professor of psychology at the Boston University School of Medicine; Elizabeth A. Harrington, Ph.D., clinical instructor in psychiatry at the Boston University School of Medicine; and Bessel A. van der Kolk, M.D., director, Massachusetts Mental Health Trauma Center and author of *Psychological Trauma* and *Post Traumatic Stress Disorder: Psychological and Biological Sequelae,* spoke at a conference entitled "Women," sponsored by the Harvard Medical School, held in June 1988, Cambridge, Massachusetts.
8. Linda Sanford and Mary Ellen Donovan, *Women and Self-Esteem,* (New York: Anchor Press/Doubleday, 1984), 3.
9. Janet Woititz, *Struggle for Intimacy,* (Deerfield Beach, Florida: Health Communications, Inc., 1985), 94.
10. Anonymous, *Each Day a New Beginning,* (Center City, Minnesota: Hazelden Foundation, 1982, January 4).
11. Carol Gilligan, *In a Different Voice,* (Cambridge: Harvard University Press, 1982), 122–123.
12. Siegel, *Love, Medicine and Miracles,* 111.
13. Miller, *Toward a New Psychology of Women,* xxi.
14. Robin Norwood, *Women Who Love Too Much,* (New York: Pocket Books, 1986), 260–261.
15. Robert Jay Lifton, *Home from War,* (New York: Simon and Schuster, 1973), 151.
16. Robert Jay Lifton, *The Broken Connection,* (New York: Simon and Schuster, 1979), 177.
17. From a paper, "The Human of the Future: The Synergistic Personality," presented by Al Sieberg at Western Psychology Association Convention, San Jose, California, April 1985.

♦ ♦ ♦

Chapter Two

1. Siegel, *Love, Medicine and Miracles,* 78.
2. Bessel A. van der Kolk, M.D., *Psychological Trauma,* (Washington, D.C.: American Psychiatric Press, 1987), 165.

Chapter Three

1. Woititz, *Struggle for Intimacy,* 14.
2. John Bradshaw, "Our Families, Ourselves," *Lears,* March 1989, 95.
3. Bass, *The Courage to Heal,* 60.
4. *Ibid,* 68, 175, 323.
5. Anonymous, *Each Day a New Beginning,* February 19.
6. Sharon Wegscheider, *Another Chance: Hope and Health for the Alcoholic Family,* (Palo Alto, California: Science and Behavior Books, Inc., 1981), 29.
7. Miller, *Toward a New Psychology of Women,* 111.

Chapter Four

1. Judith Viorst, *Necessary Losses,* (New York: Ballantine Books, 1986), 275.
2. Peck, *The Road Less Traveled,* 268
3. Sanford, *Women and Self-Esteem,* 11.
4. Mary Catherine Bateson, *Composing a Life,* (New York: The Atlantic Monthly Press, 1989), 8.
5. Anonymous, *Each Day a New Beginning,* July 5.
6. Siegel, *Love, Medicine and Miracles,* 181.

Chapter Five

1. The American Society of Addiction Medicine (ASAM) and the National Council on Alcoholism and Drug Dependence (NCADD) announced a revised definition of alcoholism, published in cooperation with Edgehill Newport, in "The Addiction Report," June 1990.
2. Beattie, *Codependent No More,* 123.
3. Woititz, *Struggle for Intimacy,* 93.
4. Viorst, *Necessary Losses,* 46–47.

♦ ♦ ♦

5. Claudia Black, *Repeat After Me,* (Denver, Colorado: M.A.C. Printing and Publications, 1985), 71.
6. Bass, *The Courage to Heal,* 359.
7. van der Kolk, *Psychological Trauma,* 155.

Chapter Six

1. Bradshaw, "Our Families, Ourselves," 98.
2. Beattie, *Codependent No More,* 31.
3. Norwood, *Women Who Love Too Much,* 235.
4. Miller, *Toward a New Psychology of Women,* 110.
5. Beattie, *Codependent No More,* 197.
6. Bateson, *Composing a Life,* 59, 62.
7. Gilligan, *In a Different Voice,* 17.
8. Lifton, *Death in Life: Survivors of Hiroshima,* 536.
9. Bass, *The Courage to Heal,* 427.

Chapter Seven

1. Beattie, *Codependent No More,* 121.
2. Norwood, *Women Who Love Too Much,* 178.
3. Sanford, *Women and Self-Esteem,* 5.
4. Grace Baruch, Rosalind Barnett, and Caryl Rivers, *Lifeprints,* (New York: McGraw Hill Book Co., 1983), 242.

Chapter Eight

1. Bradshaw, "Our Families, Ourselves," 64.
2. van der Kolk, *Psychological Trauma,* 155.
3. Fannie Flagg, "Fear of Prying: A Testimonial to Support Groups," *Lears,* May 1989, 62.
4. John Friel, Ph.D., and Linda Friel, M.A., *An Adult Child's Guide to What's "Normal,"* (Deerfield Beach, Florida: Health Communications, Inc., 1990), 31.

♦ ♦ ♦

5. Harriet Lerner, Ph.D., *The Dance of Anger,* (New York: Harper and Row, 1985), 15.
6. Miller, *Toward a New Psychology of Women,* 131.
7. Ed Fitzgerald, *That Place in Minnesota,* (New York: Viking Press, 1990), 235–237.
8. Lerner, *The Dance of Anger,* 139.
9. Viorst, *Necessary Losses,* 127.
10. Miller, *Toward a New Psychology of Women,* xx.

Chapter Nine

1. van der Kolk, *Psychological Trauma,* 133.
2. Bass, *The Courage to Heal,* 41–42.
3. Bradshaw, "Our Families, Ourselves," 86.
4. Friel, *An Adult Child's Guide to What's "Normal,"* 26.
5. Siegel, *Love, Medicine and Miracles,* 166.
6. Elizabeth Rose, *Lady of Gray: Healing Candida,* (Santa Monica, California: Butterfly Publishing Co., 1985), preface.
7. Lifton, *Death in Life: Survivors of Hiroshima,* 403.
8. *The New York Times Book Review,* Sunday, August, 19, 1990.
9. From a paper, "The Human of the Future: The Synergistic Personality," presented at Western Psychology Association Convention, San Jose, California, April, 1990.

Chapter Ten

Gail Sheehy, "The Victorious Personality," *New York Times Magazine,* Sunday, April 20, 1986, 26.